Born in 1909, Cyril Northcote Parkinson comes originally from Barnard Castle, County Durham, and was educated at St Peter's School, York, and at the Universities of Cambridge and London. Since then he has had a varied career as painter, teacher, soldier, journalist, and author. A Fellow at one time of Emmanuel College, Cambridge, he was Raffles Professor of History at the University of Malaya from 1950 to 1958. He has taught since then at Harvard, Illinois, and the University of California at Berkeley. He claims to have learnt his first lessons in administration when serving on the General Staff during World War II. All three services, however, combined to provide him with the experience upon which his first famous Law was based. He is married, with five children all told, and lives in Guernsey when not travelling, as he often does, in the U.S.A. and on the Continent.

Until *Parkinson's Law* was published in 1957 his authorship was confined to historical works such as *Trade in the Eastern Seas* (1937), *The Rise of the Port of Liverpool* (1952), and *War in the Eastern Seas* (1955). Since then his satirical works, *The Law and the Profits* (1960) and *In-Laws and Outlaws* (1962) have alternated with such serious books as *The Evolution of Political Thought* (1958) and *East and West* (1963). His most recent books are *Ponies Plot* (1965; a Puffin), *A Law Unto Themselves* (1966), *Left Luggage* (1967), *Mrs Parkinson's Law* (1968), *The Law of Delay* (1970) and *The Life and Times of Horatio Hornblower* (1970).

C. Northcote Parkinson

LEFT LUGGAGE

From Marx to Wilson

PENGUIN BOOKS

Penguin Books Ltd, Harmondsworth, Middlesex, England
Penguin Books Australia Ltd, Ringwood, Victoria, Australia

—

First published by John Murray 1967
Published in Penguin Books 1970

—

Copyright © C. Northcote Parkinson, 1967

—

Made and printed in Great Britain
by C. Nicholls & Company Ltd
Set in Intertype Granjon

TO CHRISTOPHER

CONTENTS

ACKNOWLEDGEMENTS

In the writing of this book I have had help, in research from Mr Iain Sproat. The officials of the London Library were as helpful as always in bibliography and in providing source material. The manuscript was typed most efficiently by Mrs J. K. Neill, and I have had the help I have come to expect from my sympathetic publishers. To all these I record my thanks, as also to my wife, with whom I have had the most loyal support. In so far, however, as the work is still deficient, the fault is mine. Nor do I deny that someone else could have made a better book out of the same material. What I do maintain is that the book had to be written sometime by somebody.

C.N.P.

PREFACE

THE greatness of any human society depends upon leadership; and leadership implies movement. The society must have some conscious aim; defensive merely, perhaps, in the early phases; constructive (or even aggressive) when the external pressure is less. Great contributions in thought or art have come, normally, from societies that had an obvious and external purpose. Vigorous peoples have looked outward, their literature and music being a by-product of their self-assertion. This would be true, for example, of the Greeks and Romans, of the Venetians and Portuguese, of the Spanish and the Dutch. It might be said of the British, in successive centuries, that they were resisting Spain, competing with Holland and struggling against France. Once in a position of leadership, their main effort was spent in the conquest and development of the British Empire. This phase ended with the death of Victoria. In the twentieth century the British have lost their sense of mission. Their efforts have dwindled and turned inward and all their talk has been of social progress. The energy once expended on distant colonies has been turned, at half pressure, upon English slums. Surplus revenue which might have been spent upon cruisers and colonies has been allocated to pensions and perquisites, housing and health. The word which conveniently defines this trend, observable generally in Europe, is socialism; and the inherent virtues of socialism are more often assumed than explained.

For the first half of the twentieth century and now for part of the second half as well, Britain has been governed on more or less socialist principles; the socialism of Lloyd George or Macmillan being scarcely more conservative than the liberalism of Bevan or Gaitskell. With the recent renewal of the Labour Party's mandate, we have good cause to study the theory upon which that party acts and the policies based upon that theory which the other parties are content to pursue. Central to this theory and inherent in these policies is the idea of the classless society. Resigned as they may be to salary differentials, the Labour Party leaders are opposed to a class system in which heredity and inherited wealth may give a decisive advantage to one man while imposing (at least indirectly) a decisive handicap upon another. Behind their idea of the classless society lurks the dogma of equality and the concept of fairness. Both have gone unchallenged for too long in a world where democracy is itself in decline. It is time, perhaps, to hear what is to be said on the other side.

For the sort of society in which classes definitely exist there are three arguments, and they should at least be generally known. The first centres upon the need for excellence as opposed to fairness. Where a tremendous responsibility rests upon those in high office, where a single mistake can lead to the destruction of the whole society, the over-riding need is for men endowed with intelligence, knowledge, character and courage. That all should stand an equal chance in the race for office is irrelevant to the desired result. In a country like Iceland, or even Sweden, there might be a case for electing leaders who are representative (that is typical) of the population as a whole. Where a country is actually or potentially a world power, such an argument becomes untenable. What is wanted, beyond question, is the team of men best qualified for leadership.

The second argument concerns the training for leadership which must begin at birth if it is to succeed in time. To give the same training to everybody is practically impossible and would produce, in any case, the worst results. Selection at birth which is obviously essential must tend to be on the basis of heredity, although other principles of selection need not be ruled out. Heredity means training before birth and there is much doubt and dispute about its importance as compared with training from the moment of delivery. In an urban society and a restless population the factor of heredity is underestimated, there being too few opportunities for seeing three or four generations together, whether among human beings or animals. The importance of later education is perhaps exaggerated by contrast but the two factors are difficult to separate. With heredity and training directed to the same end, the child of distinguished parents has some inherent chance of distinction. Still further to improve that chance he needs the rivalry of other children whose advantages are similar. To rob him of his potential lead the best way is to place him with the children of average background among whom he can succeed too easily. Under a system of forced equality the leaders tend to be too ignorant, too tired or too old.

The third argument is based on the need for variety in background. In the classless society the leaders are those who have risen to power through the usual channels, high examination marks leading to the right college, to the first-class degree, to the right organization and the widest publicity. In the classless society all success goes to those who are classless in the right way. A queerly colourless hierarchy is the result. It is unlikely that the modern world can do without the statisticians and economists. That they must have their place in public administration is virtually certain. There is good reason to think, however, that there should be room for other people as well. The Ministers of the Crown might include not unreasonably some men of experience in trade and war, some men of distinction in literature or the arts, some men who have travelled and some who have ridden to hounds. To have too many economists from Balliol is worse than having too many eccentrics from Eton. The classless society means mental stagnation and it is already on the way.

The case for aristocracy as a factor – though not necessarily the dominant force – in society is best illustrated, finally, by a concrete example. Take as typical a family with the unusual name of X. It was a knightly family already respectable in the Middle Ages, but we hear first of a banker called X who became a Member of Parliament, and his nephew who was knighted for his distinction in surgery. The banker's son was a clergyman, his grandson a Q.C., a landowner and an Oxford don; an authority, moreover, on ecclesiastical law. Heir to the donnish Q.C. was another barrister, educated at Winchester and New College, who reached both Parliament and Privy Council, ending as Judge of the Appeal Court and accepting a peerage with the title of Z. The first Baron Z married into a wealthy manufacturing family, two successive members of which had been knighted when Mayor of Manchester. His son therefore had a mingled descent from landowner and lawyer on the one side, from more liberal and affluent business men on the other. He went inevitably to Winchester and New College but passed on, surprisingly, to success in chemistry. He subsequently followed his ancestors to the Middle Temple and Parliament, became a K.C., a Knight and Solicitor-General, married the granddaughter of the man who invented Eno's 'Fruit Salts' and ended in the Cabinet as a man whose name had become a household word.

This is the sort of career which the classless society is designed to prevent. It includes almost every element of aristocratic and capitalistic privilege, from public school to Oxford, banking to politics, from land-ownership to law. There is the careful cross-breeding between families of differing tradition and there is a foothold moreover in the House of Lords. The Cabinet Minister who finally emerged, bred to law and politics, trained for leadership and used to responsibility, was one of the cleverest men of his day; noted, however, for his deep sense of religion, as also for the simplicity of his private life. This is the sort of biography which must now be made impossible. How are the products of the primary school to have a fair chance in competition with men whose ancestry, connexions, background and wealth give them a tremendous lead before they are even born? The argument for the classless society is not merely, remember, that the working-class candidate should also be considered, but that the aristocrat's career should be made impossible. This is the case for destroying the public schools, for taxing wealth out of existence and for levelling society to a featureless plain from which the only escape is by competitive ex-

amination. This is the excuse for looking upon the profit
motive with disapproval, and upon land-ownership with horror. Here is good reason for closing the Inns of Court, and
reason, still better, for abolishing the House of Lords. In the
classless society the aristocratic X, Cabinet Minister of an
earlier age, can have no place at all. Brilliant though he may
have been, we want no others of his sort. And yet we might
wonder, pensively, whether the country (and even the Labour Party) might not have been the poorer for his abolition.
For X – or Sir Stafford Cripps, to use his actual name – was a
man of some distinction in his day.

C. NORTHCOTE PARKINSON

Guernsey
December 1966

I

TWO NATIONS

EVERY human society must reach a point at which it is most triumphantly itself; a high summer with the April rains forgotten and with scarcely a hint yet of autumn in the air. We can think of this Augustan period as a century or decade but it is at least symbolized, sometimes, in a single year. That such a golden age has been reached or passed is more apparent, however, to the discerning tourist than to the people most nearly concerned. That other folk have passed their zenith is easy to recognize. Emotionally involved in their current politics, the modern Athenians may argue about the future of Greece. That future is of no interest, however, to anyone but themselves. Dwarfed by a tremendous past, they can do little but camp among the ruins; a fact which is at least perfectly clear to everyone else. And the more sensible Athenians will be content with what they have, remembering that there are a thousand cities with no more of a future and far less of a past. There is a similar divergence of opinion between those who regard Venice as a museum and those who remind us, plaintively, that it is the place in which they have to live. But the antiquarians are essentially right for here again the past matters more than the present or future. The same is true of Versailles, which had its heyday and can expect no other. Is it any less true of Vienna or Paris? The residents can talk, if they will, of the dynamic future, but no one else is listening. The visitors see only the splendour of Louis XIV, the high civilization of Louis XV, the triumphs of Napoleon I and the town planning of Napoleon III. The great days, it is plain, are finished.

But what of London? The British, who sense all that is grotesque in the antics of De Gaulle, are still prone to talk (hesitantly, perhaps) as if their own great days are still to

come. If we have doubts about this, however, our foreign
guests have none at all. Transatlantic visitors fascinated by
the Horse Guards do not think our half-hearted modernities
worth a second glance. New buildings tall enough to offend
in their particular context are too trifling to impress the trav-
eller. Akin to that sort of absurdity is the decision to evacuate
the Admiralty in order to create a so-called Ministry of Defence. The modernizers forget that the Royal Navy, like the
Admiralty building itself, is a relic of our great period of
history, with H.M.S. *Victory* doing for Portsmouth what the
Parthenon does for Athens. The Royal Navy is no longer the
tool of Empire but is merely the symbol of a supremacy that
is lost.

The British heyday is plainly in the past and our utopia
was last glimpsed in about 1910. A fair number of people
lived then in a prosperous and beautiful countryside. Other
folk lived in cities which were highly civilized and pleasant.
An ordered society could look back complacently – perhaps
too complacently – on centuries of expansion and conquest.
The time had come for good humour and gentleness. James
Barrie had written *Peter Pan* in 1904. A. A. Milne became
assistant editor of *Punch* in 1906. Kenneth Grahame typi-
fied the age when he wrote *The Wind in the Willows* in
1908; H. G. Wells' novel *The History of Mr Polly* came out
in 1910; Max Beerbohm's *Zuleika Dobson* in 1911 and
Bernard Shaw's *Pygmalion* was produced in 1912. Looking
back, we feel that it was always summer then; a summer as
painted by Claude Shepperson and enjoyed by E. V. Lucas.
Any touch there might be of autumn was represented by
'Saki' Munro, who foresaw, uncannily, what the future
might hold. But he was exceptional, and H. G. Wells looked
more typically to a wonderful future, to a world purified by
science in which men might live as gods. By 1916 his Mr
Britling was looking back on the world he had lost, on a
generation which nothing could replace. We have never recovered since then and there is no reason to suppose that
recovery was even possible. We realize now, moreover, that
British momentum had been lost before that. After the golden

days of June would follow the wet evenings of November. After *Pygmalion* there would come *Journey's End*.

Our picture of the England of 1910 centres partly on London and partly on the English village; on the London, that is, of *My Fair Lady* and the village, shall we say, of Matchings Easy. The West End was not jammed then with motor traffic nor disfigured by concrete and glass. All was still on a human scale, the shutters painted, the door-knockers polished and the steps newly swept and whitened. Polished leather and steel caught the morning sun in Rotten Row, well-groomed horses trotted down St James's and the neater carriages drew up opposite Asprey's and Brown's. A thousand nursemaids drew the blinds in a thousand nurseries and a hundred prams converged on Kensington Gardens. On the same afternoon, at Matchings Easy, the village cricket team is about to begin its innings against the Blandings Castle eleven. The rector, in his faded blazer, watches his curate face the bowling, while the greengrocer, umpiring, stands ready to call 'Not out!'. The innkeeper warns the blacksmith against the cunning of the visiting team's slow bowler. The rooks are cawing in the rectory elms. There will be tea on the lawn at the manor, where one of these new-fangled motor cars is spluttering up the drive. Stands the church clock at ten to three? It does indeed, but the time, for all these folk round the village green, is later than they think. Rupert Brooke's Grantchester is already doomed. In the significant words chosen by A. A. Milne for the title of his autobiography '*It's too late now*'.

But while some dwelt in arcadia, others did not. The less fortunate part of Britain, the other nation, was not merely socially but geographically distinct. The unluckiest of the poor did *not* live, like Eliza Doolittle, in a London tenement but somewhere else altogether, northward, north-westward, out of sight. This was the world of the industrial slum, the background to most of our current thinking. It was created, for the most part, by the Industrial Revolution which took place in about 1870. Economic historians would have us believe that it began a century before, and so it did; but the beginnings did not revolutionize urban life. Its later and full development did so in three ways. First of all, the hours of work were appallingly lengthened. In the countryside people had always worked for as long each day as was practicable, Sundays and holidays excepted. There was leisure, however, due to darkness, frost and snow; to conditions generally which made some work impossible. Countrymen had often to wait for the right weather or season just as seamen may have to wait for the tide. The gaslit factory and office made it possible to work round the clock and this was practically what our ancestors tried to do. Second, the housing conditions and population densities which were more or less tolerable as applied to a small town were now extended to industrial centres where no town, properly speaking (and no municipal government), had ever existed. Third, the new urban areas became so extensive that the countryside was effectively out of reach. A walk out of Manchester merely brought you into Salford; a walk out of Bradford ending merely in Leeds. Children could grow up in a slum from which there was no escape. People could die without ever having left the slum; without knowing that there was any other way in which to live. Whether they realized the fact or not, a whole mass of people had been trapped in hell.

Before the coming of the industrial towns, people could live in the city or the country. In cities previously fortified the population could be unhealthily crowded. The city, however, had a life and character of which its citizens could be proud. It centred on cathedral or castle. It had a guildhall and mansion house, assize court and theatre. It had its mayor and aldermen, its clergymen and gentry, its garrison and racecourse, its market and jail. Life's monotony might be broken there by an election or murder trial, a circus or riot. And, apart from that, there were ways of escape. Perhaps an hour away on foot was the open country with flowers to pick from the hedgerow and the song of birds in the trees. Even London was small enough to allow Jorrocks (in 1838) his day's hunting over the Surrey fields. Many cities could offer, in addition, the riverside and the quay, the bustle of the shipping and the cry of the gulls. Even coasters might be bound for a foreign port, the mere name of which would hint at a wider world. There may always have been slum-dwellers in Canterbury and Bristol, Salisbury and York, but they were not imprisoned in their slum. They could look inwards to the life of the city's centre and outwards to the life of the open road, the hills and the sea.

Living in the country meant normally the life of the village; sometimes that of the market town which was only the village writ large. There was nothing necessarily idyllic about rural life as seen from the cottage or workhouse. Men might resent the parson's patronage as much as boys might wince from the farmer's whip. There are agricultural plains which are dull and hills that are forbidding and dark. But the country at its worst has something to offer if it is only the sky overhead and the smell of the hay. And one thing it has always offered is the prospect of escape to the market town, and of escape from there to the city. Helping take pigs to market has always been a first step towards freedom; if only perhaps the freedom to enlist. Mixed farming also offers a variety of work with the rhythm of animal life superimposed on the seasonal work of the fields. Life could be harsh and hard but the tasks might at least vary from feeding the sheep to digging a ditch, from thatching the dairy to mending a gate. On the bleakest of remote fells there was the additional excitement of the emergency: the hailstorm during the lambing, the sheep buried in the snow. Monotony there might be as from year to year, but British country life has never been monotonous from day to day.

The industrial slum was thus a new thing in kind, a hell from which there was no obvious escape. Upon the mean and endless streets was slammed down, as the final touch, a low ceiling of industrial filth. With that lid a permanent feature of their lives, folk no longer saw the sky; nor can they even now. For people so trapped by Giant Despair the possibilities were few. They could anaesthetize themselves with alcohol. They could seek the consolations of religion. Gambling, they could dream of the lucky chance which would waft them to happiness. They could join a trade union in the hope of gaining a higher wage. They could form a Co-operative Society with the object of making the same wage go further. They could join a political movement in the hope of creating a better world. For an almost negligible minority there was the path of promotion from charge-hand to foreman, from foreman to supervisor and from there into the ranks of management. This last line of escape implied, however, a superhuman effort in self-education; a confined explosion which might suffice to project some grandson into the House of Lords. Among people with only limited energy left after working hours, the natural Tories would drink or gamble, those of more Liberal views could combine, discuss, co-operate and pray.

The original emphasis was on prayer. Most industrial centres were in roundhead country; where manufacturers and methodism went together. Chapels might be colourless but the worshippers filled their minds with drama and light, with visions of a golden heaven and glimpses of a scarlet hell. Seeking to escape from Bruddersford at its worst, you could drink yourself out on a Saturday night or think yourself out on a Sunday morning. The alcoholic was thus twelve hours ahead. The Methodist had more, however, for his money; for he added to the satisfaction of being 'saved' the happy knowledge that his noisier neighbours were undoubtedly damned. As clearly destined for eternal torment were the directors of the company, the manager, the parson and the squire. Things were to work out fairly in the end. In the meanwhile the Methodist could indulge in the pleasures of disapproval. Nor were these inconsistent with certain of the alternative ways of escape; the trade union method and the political method. It was indeed the Methodist sermon which turned itself into the political oration or the trade union appeal. Common to both was the resentment felt against those who refused to join, the 'blackleg' being the secular equivalent of the unregenerate and the word 'chapel' having a meaning outside the strictly religious context. In what had been always roundhead country, the religious-political atmosphere prevailed, the public house being the resort of a minority – with a back door often available, however, to those who dared not be seen at the front.

Consigned to hell in this world, the more respectable poor consigned their 'betters' to hell in the next. Their reaction was natural enough. Their mistake (natural again) was to suppose that their own immediate fate was the result of deliberate policy. Deliberate it had never been but callous it certainly was. The eighteenth century, when the original mistakes had been made, was a tough period in British history; more harsh perhaps than the Middle Ages had ever been. Indifference to individual suffering was partly the result of the external effort being made. With so much at stake – the future for example of America, Australia, Canada and India – little attention was paid to the town-planning of Huddersfield or Leeds. There was the same atmosphere in the United States when the westward movement was at its height. Families could perish by the wayside but they were regarded as expendable and probably to blame for their own misfortune. And, apart from that, casualties leave something to hand out among the survivors and fewer to share the final spoils. Where we are wrong, in retrospect, is to see the cotton spinners and coal miners as the only victims of the process. Men were just as callous in the colonies or at sea. The aristocrats were just as ruthless, for that matter, among themselves. When the army is advancing rapidly the wounded are often left to die. Their chance is sometimes better in a siege or even during a withdrawal. For one thing, they are more likely to be seen; for another, they may be regarded as valuable. Florence Nightingale's chance at Sevastopol arose from the fact that the campaign had been brought to a standstill. She could have done nothing for Wellington's army at Vittoria and no one would have noticed it if she had. Humanitarianism begins when we have time for it; after our momentum has been lost.

When Britain's external influence was at its height, the landscape was already divided between the Two Nations as defined in Disraeli's novel of 1845. But the strength of Britain had derived from combining the two. In British society there were no rigid barriers dividing the nobility from the gentry or the gentry from the middle class. Agriculture was linked with industry and both with commerce. Church and university were linked with politics and both again with law. There was a contrast, to be sure, between the southern counties and the coalfields, and indeed between Liverpool and Manchester, but all had worked for the same purpose: the defeat of France and the expansion of Britain. It was the diversity of the means which made the ends attainable. All opposition was overwhelmed by frigates and diplomacy, by textiles and rum. The Duke of Wellington and John Wesley were not only allies but distant relatives. To any given problem the means applied might vary from naval intervention to financial subsidy, from the gospel to gun-running and from trade to war. In the great period of British expansion, the effort came from people who were oddly contrasted and yet surprisingly agreed. The public schools, a late development, were only a minor factor in the process but they came to symbolize the unity of leadership. The final result was to ensure that the aristocrat and the business man, the lawyer and the civil servant, the army officer and the merchantman's captain, had all been at much the same sort of school. Whether they had learnt anything from this experience, and whether what they learnt would be relevant to their probable career might be a matter for dispute. What they did gain, beyond question, was a reliance on each other's loyalty and courage. A typical instrument of British policy was the East India Company, in which the various elements of British society were knit together for the intertwined purposes of trade and war. It is futile to look back in anger on all the Company achieved. The campaign may be more or less finished but we are ourselves the product, steeped in a tradition which has fashioned our lives from the wearing of pyjamas to the drinking of tea. We cannot turn our backs a past which is also the present, on fathers who were so like ourselves.

The Two Nations of 1845 produced two kinds of history,

one of which has died out and the other survives. We had, first of all, the school history which centred upon 'Deeds which Won the Empire'; a saga which included all battles from Agincourt to Waterloo. There has since grown up, from about 1900, the school history which centres upon 'The Life of the Common People'; a lament for proletarian hardships from the Enclosures to the Dole. By consistent emphasis on social progress it becomes possible nowadays to forget about the battles and dwell mainly upon agriculture; a subject about which the urban teacher is of course completely ignorant. What the children learn, if anything, may be immaterial; what they are seldom taught is that the Cavalier and Roundhead traditions in English life are of equal importance and that destruction of either means the destruction of both. What they fail to learn in class, however, they often manage to learn in play. For Britain is, significantly, the country where most team games have originated. We pick sides almost automatically, pitting one group against another. We play for our side, moreover, and we play to win. Whatever our excitement, however, and however strong our will to victory, we never seek to destroy the other side. Without opponents, we realize, our own team could not even exist.

Each team depends upon its opposite. We may agree among ourselves at Cambridge that Oxford is a deplorable place where dons profess an old-fashioned type of socialism, where undergraduates are either too aesthetic or too hearty, where learning is pretentious and women too much in evidence. We look with pity on people who read Modern Greats as a preliminary to a career in Westminster, Whitehall, Fleet Street or the B.B.C. We turn from All Souls with a shudder and have no wish to see anything even remotely similar at Cambridge. But were anyone to go further and propose that Oxford should be abolished, our opposition would be immediate. That, we should feel, is going too far. Without Oxford there could be no Boat Race. No one, without Oxford, could earn so much as a half-blue for lacrosse or archery. To have more than two universities in England might be thought absurd, but to have only one seems hardly feasible. Without Oxford, we have to admit, Cambridge would be something other than the Cambridge we have known. And this, we come to realize, is true of other institutions. England needs Scotland, Guernsey needs Jersey, Yorkshire needs Lancashire, the *Worcester* needs the *Conway,* the Lifeguards need the Horseguards and the detectives need the criminals. Abolish our opponents and we cease to be ourselves.

Our need is not merely for a rival but for an opponent who can win. While hoping for victory in any given contest, we know that to win every time would be monotonous. Such a consistent result would lead, in fact, to the event being abandoned altogether. Should Eton beat Harrow in twelve successive matches, the question would arise as to whether Harrow could be regarded any longer as a proper opponent. The same general principles have applied to British politics for the last 250 years. The opposing parties have sought victory in each general election; they have not sought the destruction of the other side. The idea has come, in fact, to prevail that the alternation of the two parties in office is essential to the British system of parliamentary government. It has been generally agreed, moreover, that the struggle for office has some real advantages, more especially when the two sides are of at least comparable strength. All depends, however, upon the moderation shown by each party during its term of office. Any one move made to weaken the opposition could end this unwritten agreement and with it the whole system to which it is basic. Brought up on team games, the British think of politics in terms of cricket. Each side has its innings during which the other side must field. Were the innings of either side prolonged indefinitely or were the batsman to attack the wicket-keeper, a game of some sort might be possible; but it would not be cricket.

The sudden movement of those whose resolve was to escape from the slum gave a powerful support to the general cause of what was called Liberalism. But the movement brought with it a bitterness which had long been absent from politics. Leaders who emerged from the slum saw that the rest of England was vastly more pleasant. They felt a savage resentment against the economic tyranny under which they had to live. It was not merely a question of there being two nations but of the one being dependent on the other. The portly parson and sporting squire were not, for the most part, living on incomes derived from agriculture. Their investments were in an industry of which they saw little but the dividends. Nor would their pleasant country life have been otherwise possible. The idea of the average village having a resident lord of the manor is purely Victorian and implies a background of industry. In terms of agricultural income it had always taken several manors to support a squire and hundreds to support a Peer of the Realm. The prosperity of many a nineteenth-century village was due to the squire taking nothing from it and putting a great deal in. His real income came not from farms but from factories. Just as the slum had been necessary to earlier victories by land and sea, so it had become essential to the later tradition of benevolent land ownership. The best kind of rural landlord was the man whose income came from somewhere else.

Discontent with the life of the slum became explosive in the later nineteenth century. The movement would have been ineffective, nevertheless, had the more fortunate people been as callous as they were often believed to be. Up to a point they had governed confidently, never doubting the excellence of their heritage. Western civilization was triumphant and Britain's leadership of the West was quite widely accepted. British institutions were the models to be copied and British ideas were those in vogue. Among the educated Victorians few questioned the value of a classical education. Fewer saw anything amiss with Christianity, or the Bank of England, the Royal Academy or the House of Lords. Things virtually above criticism ranged from the Royal Navy to the National Debt, from the Royal Yacht Squadron to the Jockey Club. Orthodoxy was among the highest virtues and blasphemy among the blackest crimes. Quite suddenly, however, the mood changed. Confidence gave way to hesitation and certainty gave place to doubt. And the first institution to come under scrutiny was the one most basic to traditional and rural society; the Church of England itself. The Gothic Revival of about 1845, paralleled by the Tractarian Movement, was revolutionary. It attacked the very pillars of society, threw doubts on the Reformation and foreshadowed (as it seemed) the return to Rome. Changes in ritual or the style of architecture might not be important in themselves. What they symbolized, however, was a sudden loss of direction. For if the British had been wrong about the Renaissance and the Reformation who was to say that they were right about anything else? They were less consistent, in that case, than the Portuguese or the Irish. What right had they to rule over an oriental world to which they were returning in fact for inspiration? After some generations of vigorous policy based upon the firmest self-confidence, some of the British began to waver. They wavered in about 1840 to 1850 and their wavering coincided with the publication (in 1848) of the *Communist Manifesto*. The British momentum had begun to slacken. In another fifty years or so it would be lost.

2

THE REVOLT

DISCONTENT with the life of the industrial slum led some to gamble, some to drink, and a few into self-help and success. For the majority, however, of the urban working class the line of escape lay through nonconformity into trade union-ism and co-operation and so from there into politics. To appreciate what was achieved in this way one has to realize that the story in other countries was entirely different. No development of this sort was possible against a Catholic back-ground. It was not inevitable, for that matter, against any background. There has been nothing comparable, for ins-tance, in the United States. Only in Britain did the revolt take this particular form; perhaps because of Methodist in-fluence upon the early trade unions. These were formed, in the first place, by respectable and religious men. The fam-ily background which people had lost when moving from the countryside into the town was replaced by an organiza-tion which would at once absorb and protect the individual. The trade union did not at first represent poverty as against the tyranny of wealth, for some early unions were formed among skilled workmen, like printers, whose pay was rela-tively good. Similar top hats were worn (at least on Sunday) by the well-paid shipwright and the ill-paid bank clerk, the difference between them being that the trade union member did not even want to be regarded as a gentleman. He was more often a nonconformist who looked upon the gentry with the deepest disapproval. His current respectability, whe-ther attained or desired, reflected above all the approval of God. Neatness and cleanliness might be an object, but to aim at anything more might be thought worldly and vain. Although there were trade disputes and strikes before 1800, the Trade Union Movement is essentially Victorian in atmosphere. Of 47 major unions existing in 1918, the majority had been formed between 1830 and 1900, 14 between 1830 and 1850, 17 between 1850 and 1880; the oldest dated from 1809 and the latest from 1902.

Some of the earliest trade unions were in the London area. It was there, and among the highly skilled trades, that the problems of organization were first encountered and eventually solved. Later union constitutions were all to be based on that of the Amalgamated Society of Engineers. As against that, the Miners' Association of Great Britain and Ireland, formed at Wakefield in 1843, was an amalgamation of the unions existing in Northumberland and Durham, Lancashire and Yorkshire. This foreshadowed the move northward between 1851 and 1863, which shifted the weight of the movement into the counties north of the Humber and Dee. These contained at least 726,000 union members by 1892. The greatest numbers were in Lancashire, London, and the West Riding, the numbers highest in proportion to population were in Northumberland and Durham. The industrial Midlands, with South Wales, accounted for much of the remaining strength. Total membership came to a million and a half by that period, comprising about 20 per cent of the adult, male, manual-working and wage-earning populace. Unions were formed by this time among the less skilled and less highly paid groups of wage-earners. These 'New Unions' as they were called, existed among the dockers and seamen and were regarded with considerable alarm. There were no unions even then for the really poor.

Trade unions were not, in the nineteenth century, associated with any political party. The majority of the members were Liberal, no doubt, but many would have seen little to choose, from their point of view, between Gladstone and Disraeli. It was Gladstone's government which passed the Trade Union Act of 1871, legalizing and defining the unions' position. It was under Disraeli that the Conspiracy and Protection of Property Act was passed, in which peaceful picketing was made lawful. The unions' legal position seemed secure, and the more so in that, not being legal corporations, they could not (it was thought) be sued for damages in their corporate capacity. As from about 1890 legal and public opinion turned against them, and a Royal Commission on Labour recommended in 1894 that any union should be held responsible at law for any tortious acts committed on its behalf. Without any legislative change the courts began to interpret the existing law in that sense. In 1900 the employees of the Taff Vale Railway Company, in South Wales, went on strike. The Company promptly sued the Amalgamated Society of Railway Servants. Rather to everyone's surprise, Mr Justice Farwell allowed the Company £23,000 in damages, the Union being also liable to pay £42,000 in costs. This judgement was upheld in the House of Lords (July 1901), their Lordships deciding that the Union, while not a corporation, had nevertheless a corporate liability. The unions found themselves in a dangerous position from which only legislation could save them. They began, as from this time, to move into politics.

The Tory government of 1895–1905 was led until 1901 by the Marquess of Salisbury. A series of incidents, from the West End Riots of 1886 to the London Dock Strike of 1889, gave him public support against the trade unions. He used force when necessary and was prepared to use more. His show of strength was the Liberals' cue to side with the working class. Left-wing Liberals had been vociferous since 1889. Their pressure now increased, with demands for social reform, local government reform, free education and subsidized housing. They also sought to disestablish and disendow the Established Church in Scotland and Wales. One effect of this movement was to emphasize the nonconformist character of the trade union membership. Co-operation with the more radical Liberals meant alliance with the chapel. And while the Liberals failed, in the long run, to capture the trade unions for their own party, they did succeed in destroying such contact as the unions may have had with the Tories. Chapel influence in the trade unions has been, of course, extremely valuable. It served, nevertheless, to emphasize the narrowness of the unions' outlook. As contrasted with the middle-class associations, which are concerned mainly with status, the trade unions have concentrated from the outset on wages.

The weakness in trade union policy lay from the outset in its lack of idealism. The union leaders did not point the way to any ideal form of society. They merely wanted to see wage levels raised to the highest point which the employers could afford. This sort of demand was natural enough but it had no moral basis. It gave the worker no right to point the finger of scorn at the capitalist, whose motives were no more material and whose methods were broadly the same. To sell what you have to offer, whether goods or services, at the highest possible price is no crime against humanity; that being, within limits, what we all do. But our efforts to this end cannot be made to look particularly progressive or noble. There are sound reasons for selling anything at the maximum price, any other policy being foolish and often corrupt, but this practice can scarcely be raised to the ethical level of the Lord's Prayer. It is not even a principle for which many of us would be prepared to die in battle. Morally considered, it stands on a par with the buyers' urge to buy at the lowest possible price. The Co-operative Movement stands, to that extent, on the same level as the Trade Union Movement. When we read, therefore, about 'the Bethlehem of democratic Co-operation' we sense all that is incongruous in such an expression. To buy one's groceries cheap is no more idealistic than to sell one's labour dear; nor does it obviously entitle us to look down from any moral height on the grocer who asks as much as his customers will pay and pays as little as his assistants will accept.

The crude economics of Co-operation do not, however, tell the whole story. For the movement was imbued at the outset with an idealism which the trade unions lacked. This was because the co-operators had something positive to do. The existence of the trade union depends, by contrast, upon having an employer to fight – without whom the union must disintegrate. The pioneers of Co-operation did not depend upon the same sort of antagonism. Their task was something immediate, something practical and something in which everyone could share. The enemy in so far as there was one might be ignored rather than fought; and the movement had aims which were not purely economic. This was because the founders of the movement were, some of them, followers of Robert Owen (1771–1858), the social reformer. Owen's factory at New Lanark was the scene of a social experiment which included non-profit-making stores. This example inspired William Cooper and Charles Howarth to found the first successful venture in co-operative trading. This was the Rochdale Store, opened in Toad Lane, Rochdale, in December 1844, with twenty-eight members.

This first Society was an association of consumers who thought to secure goods cheaply by eliminating the shopkeeper's profit. According to Owen, the profit upon cost price is the essence of original sin, the root cause of misery and greed. On this principle, goods should have been sold at cost price, but that was found to be impracticable. The plan adopted was therefore to sell at the market price but divide the profit among the customers, who were also originally the owners, in proportion to the amount they had spent. The original store was a success and the movement spread to other parts of Lancashire; to Bacup, Todmorden, Leigh, Salford, Padiham and Middleton. From Lancashire it spread into Yorkshire and so to the Scottish Lowlands, to the Midlands, to Northumberland and Durham. The first conference of the movement was held at Rochdale in 1850, and further discussion led to the formation (in 1863) of the North of England Co-operative Wholesale Society, the buying organization which would enable the stores to benefit from bulk purchase. By 1893 there were 1200 associations with a membership of 993,000. Co-operative enterprise was afterwards extended to coal, milk, banking, insurance, printing, travel agency and funerals. Of the general success of the movement there can be no question at all.

From the point of view of the present work, there are four significant features of the Co-operative Movement; its original atmosphere, its partial failure, its geographical territory and its educational mission. Its atmosphere, to begin with, was religious, high-minded and prim. Whereas a trade union could be regarded as unpatriotic, seditious, conspiratorial and secret, there was nothing in the Rochdale experiment to which the squire or vicar could object. Local tradesmen might fume, but the Chapel could only approve. For what the housewife might save on her purchases was not available for her husband to spend on liquor. And the further objects of the movement were admirable, the Rochdale Store having a newsroom and library as from 1849 to which members contributed twopence a month. There was a laboratory, even, with microscopes available on loan, and evening lectures on science and art. So respectable were the pioneers that the movement had the active support of Mr Tom Hughes, Barrister-at-Law, M.P., author of *Tom Brown's Schooldays* (1857) and leader, with Charles Kingsley, of the Christian Socialist Movement. This intellectual atmosphere helped the Co-operatives to obtain legal protection. Registered at first as Friendly Societies, they were specifically recognized in the Act of 1852. There followed a battle over their liability to pay income tax, the Co-operatives refusing to pay as from 1856 and being exempt from 1862. Even the members' dividends were exempt from 1876, the idea being that a Co-operative Association is virtuous by definition and mentally linked with education, temperance and thrift. It is not even specifically lower-class, the Civil Service and Army and Navy Stores being middle-class equivalents. Its legal advantages were, in fact, to survive its cultural pretensions; more especially in certain of the countries to which the movement spread.

Where the British Co-operatives largely failed was on the manufacturing side. The founders of the movement were not merely starting, as they thought, a co-operatively owned chain of grocery and drapery stores. They were pointing the way to a practical utopia. Instead of grousing about low wages and high prices, the wage-earners were to set up rival factories and stores of their own. By becoming their own employers and suppliers, they would found a new type of community. They would end with their own newspapers, libraries, schools and colleges. Instead of fighting the capitalist structure of industry, they would quietly supersede it by virtue of the freedom in which all the lawyers and economists believed. Producers' Co-operatives began with the Peoples' Mill at Leeds and began to multiply. Then they ran into difficulties, dwindling in number until, by 1882, there were only twenty left. They recovered later but in a new form as adjuncts to the Consumers' Associations, as Co-operative factories under C.W.S. control, specializing in textiles, clothing, boots and shoes. It was one thing, in fact, to produce for a closed market; quite another to compete against private enterprise. Why was this? Because the wage-earner cannot afford to lose money. To invest in a grocer's shop to which its customers are bound by financial interest and ideological loyalty is not a business risk. To sell boots on the open market is something entirely different. The boots can remain unsold, irrespective of their quality or price, retailers preferring not to handle them or potential customers being out of work. The co-operative workmen can be left without their wages and in debt, moreover, for rent and fuel. This is not the sort of risk a man is even entitled to take, with his family to consider. If it is morally questionable for the working man to risk on the racecourse the money which is needed for food, it is far worse for him to risk in business the money which he does not even possess. The tradesman has to ask himself regularly, 'How much can I afford to lose?' In reply to this question the wage-earner, by contrast, must normally say, 'Nothing,' and would be wrong to answer in any other way. The risks of the market are not for him.

The geography of the Co-operative movement is one of its most interesting features. It began as we have seen, in Rochdale, north of Manchester; where Bolton, Oldham, Bradford and Huddersfield are all within 25 miles, with Leeds and Sheffield but little farther. This is all roundhead country, industrial, methodist, dirty and grim. The pioneers of Rochdale kept the movement non-political, but its support came from the Liberal side, and it was to roundhead country that the Co-ops appealed. By 1880 the strength of the movement centred upon Leeds, Manchester, Rochdale, Bury, Bolton and Oldham. By 1900 it had spread to Plymouth, Edinburgh, Newcastle and London, gaining ground afterwards in Birmingham, Liverpool and Bristol. There has been little success in rural England to the west and south, and still less in Ireland, Wales, Cornwall or the Highlands. The mixture of moral idealism and commercial shrewdness which appeals to some people is slightly nauseating to others. What is acceptable in Halifax and Barnsley is rejected without hesitation in Brecon or Truro. The oratory of the Co-operative Congress, bearing little or no relationship to what is actually done, has less effect in Glasgow than in Edinburgh, more influence in Aberdeen than Cork. To shop at the Co-op is and has always been an act of faith more than a matter of choice. It is just consistent with voting Conservative but not with wearing an old school tie. In general the Co-op shopper keeps to the left.

After we have read of the Co-operative successes in wholesale purchase and retail distribution, the accompanying talk about uplift must seem a little incongruous. What has all this to do with 'human fellowship', industrial democracy and the 'free ministering of all by all'? How could anyone call this 'the economic basis for the future religion of humanity'? What justification there is must lie in the educational activities of the movement, which were conspicuous, as we have seen, in the early days. But these activities died away to a point in 1882 when they amounted to nothing. Four years later the Leeds Society voted something for educational work – ¾ of 1%. The Co-operative Congress of 1898 was even more enlightened, no less than £60,000 being spent by 1900. All efforts in this direction were finally divided between the Workers' Educational Association, formed at Oxford in 1903, and the Co-operative College, founded near Manchester in 1919. The W.E.A. owed much to Co-operation and to Albert Mansbridge, its second branch being opened at Rochdale itself. It came to be run in conjunction with the Extra-Mural Departments set up at the universities from about

1873. Essence of the W.E.A. tutorial class is that it extends over three winter sessions, each weekly lecture being followed by an hour's discussion. Although some of the first classes were at Rochdale, with R. H. Tawney as tutor, they were more sponsored than financed by the C.W.S. and have gradually become just an aspect of adult education. They retain a leftish character, more especially at their summer schools, but make no great impact on the community as a whole. In so far, moreover, as the W.E.A. is supposed to console people for the secondary education they have missed, it is made obsolete by the process which has extended secondary education to all.

The trade unions and Co-operative Societies could never, by themselves, have overturned Society. To sell your labour dear and buy your groceries cheap is not a step towards revolution. And the working class, using these two kinds of organization, was well within the framework of Victorian theory. Free trade was the accepted ideal and it extended logically to the union lodge and the Rochdale store. The freedom of speech in which many Victorians believed was as applicable to the printers' chapel as to the Methodist church. Nor would the Victorian artisans, left to themselves, have had any clear idea of the world they were trying to create. Many had their eyes fixed on a future life, with a place in heaven for themselves and in hell for the foreman. Trade unionists who wanted 'More' were seldom minded to ask instead for 'All', and while the co-operators told each other about the Co-operative Commonwealth, it was an ideal towards which they made no perceptible progress. Plans for the reform of society came not from the industrial slum but from people born outside it; from people to whom the slum, when they saw it, came as a shock. Socialist theory was mostly the work of the educated and affluent.

In studying the history of revolt we find that it seldom occurs, and still more rarely succeeds, under a regime that is sure of itself. Our first mental picture may be of brave men plotting against a crushing tyranny, against a ruthless and cruel despot, against an exclusive group of the heartless and the proud. We soon realize, however, that men are not as brave as that. They do not rebel against strength and cruelty but against weakness and indecision. Revolutions take place when the regime is wavering and, above all, divided. Nor was the British Revolution an exception to this rule. It began when the aristocracy faltered, uncertain of its destiny. It began, to be precise, between 1840 and 1850. It began with the Gothic Revival.

Why? The answer may not be obvious, but the Gothic Revival had, from the beginning, its political and social implications. More than that, the two movements – to revive the arts of the Middle Ages and to rescue the working class from the industrial slum – began with much the same people at much the same time. The Gothic reconstruction of the Houses of Parliament began in 1840. Ruskin went on his epoch-making travels and saw Venice for the first time in 1841. This was the year in which Thomas Carlyle turned from his study of Chartism to publish *Heroes and Hero Worship,* which led on to *Past and Present* in 1843. Pugin's English Monastery (the first for three centuries) was consecrated in 1844. John Henry Newman was received into the Catholic Church in 1845, his Tractarian followers remaining to Catholicize the Church of England. William Morris's father died in 1847, leaving him free to do very much as he chose. Another clergyman, Charles Kingsley, declared himself a Christian Socialist in 1848 – the year after Karl Marx had drafted the *Communist Manifesto* – and Ruskin published *The Seven Lamps of Architecture* in 1849. By the end of the decade the Gothic Revival, the Co-operative Movement, the Anglo-Catholic Church and the doctrines of Socialism were all established in Britain, not by chance coincidence but as different aspects of the same idea. Essence of this idea was a rejection of everything for which Britain had stood. A world of contract was to be replaced by a world of status.

In Britain of the Industrial Revolution the theory had been that each man had to look after himself and his family. If he could not support his children, it was his own fault for having married. When the Cornish tin-mining industry collapsed, the miners did not march through London in protest. They went overseas in search of tin, some Malayan mines still having their registered office in Redruth. The current theory, and often the practice, was based upon that sturdy independence which governed the growth of nineteenth-century America. Samuel Smiles did not publish *Self-help* until 1859, but he was expressing an orthodoxy which can be traced back to Daniel Defoe. The minority which now cried: 'Back to the Middle Ages!' were not only rejecting the Renaissance and the Reformation. They were expressing their preference for a society in which the individual would matter less and the community count for more. To the upper middle-class thinker, appalled by the industrial slum, the medieval structure of society had a great appeal. The peasant or workman had a secure position in manor or guild and an opportunity for self-expression through religion and art. Some common beliefs about the Middle Ages we know to have been mistaken. In general, however, the point of view was tenable. Looking back on two Englands, the one that had produced the cathedrals and the other that had produced the country houses (and slums), it was not unreasonable to prefer the first. This would mean a rejection, however, of Britain's world leadership and a rejection, eventually, of western world supremacy.

However attractive the Middle Ages might seem in retrospect, it was still a question whether a return to them was feasible. Easiest to bring about was the replacement of the Palladian by the Gothic in architecture. Even in this, however, the elevations were easier to alter than the plans. And while a railway station can be designed in a medieval (or oriental) style, the railway itself remains obstinately Victorian and can hardly be anything else. As for society as a whole its structure was as intractable as the railway system on which it had come to depend. To do anything drastic would involve the dictatorial powers which Napoleon III was applying to the layout of Paris. In his doctrine of hero-worship, drawn from the mists of Teutonic legend, Carlyle reveals his awareness of this fact. Middle-class reformers were thus faced at the outset by the opposition not only of the factory owners but of the workmen. The reformers came to realize, some sooner and some later, that the lower classes cannot be rescued from the slum unless they will do as they are told. This, they came to see, is a basic principle of existence. You cannot help an old woman to cross a busy street unless she will accept your guidance. The very act of going to the rescue makes you superior to the person rescued. And just as folk in danger must obey the orders of the lifeboatman or fireman, the victims of the industrial slum must follow the social reformer's advice. That they are incapable of saving themselves is the most obvious result of their ill-treatment. Kindly but firmly they must be shown the way to escape. A better environment can be theirs but only if they will obey orders. It is this kindly coercion that has come to be known as Socialism.

Attracted as some of them were by the medieval structure of society the social reformers came to see that its reconstruction was impossible. They gradually turned to Political Economy, as expounded from 1844 by John Stuart Mill. The crisis for John Ruskin, one of the most influential authors of the day, came in about 1860. Most of his work until then was about medieval architecture and modern art. *Unto This Last* marked a change in direction which led to *Fors Clavigera* (1871) and to Ruskin's championship of the working man. Still more significant, however, is the conversion of William Morris. He worked only as painter and poet from 1857 to about 1883, gaining a tremendous reputation in either field. Understanding the Middle Ages more than Ruskin ever did, he brought about a revolution in the arts and crafts. He taught that the artist's work extends to textiles and ceramics, to wallpaper and books. He proved that something of the medieval tradition could be adapted to the world of industry. And when he turned to socialism, after 1883, his views were characteristically illustrated in *The Dream of John Bull* (1888) and in *News from Nowhere* (1891). His medievalism had at least this advantage, that he could paint a vivid picture of the society he wanted. A return to the Middle Ages meant, for him, a return to the simplicities of the village life, a recovery of the joys of craftmanship and a recapture of everything colourful from a past age of imagined happiness and romance. We are left, as one critic remarked, with 'the decorative arts, open-air exercise, and an abundance of beautiful and innocent girls'. The idealized Pre-Raphaelite woman has, it is true, a pensive look, but this is due (it is now supposed) less to her doubts about medieval sanitation than to the fact that Morris's wife and model would rather have married Dante Gabriel Rossetti. Be that as it may, Morris saw that art is the test of civilization. He also believed, for a time, that socialism would free the arts. He was an active socialist for about seven years, speaking on behalf of the Democratic Federation, which was associated in turn with the Land Reform Union, the National Secular Society, the Scottish Land and Labour League and the (East London) Labour Emancipation League. These groups differed a great deal in their aspirations but were sufficiently united to organize a procession to the grave of Karl Marx in March 1884. Marx had died the year before, his reputation (such as it was) resting upon the publication of the first volume of *Das Kapital* in the German edition of 1867. The other two volumes came out posthumously in 1885 and 1894, there being no English translation until 1907. The crucial episode, for Morris, was the Trafalgar Square Riot of 1886. The cowardice of his socialist friends on that occasion left him disillusioned. He turned to other things, to the writing of his long prose romances and to the organization of the Kelmscott Press. He was none the less a socialist to the end, dreaming of a society 'in which there should be neither rich nor poor, neither master nor master's man, neither idle nor overworked, neither brain-sick brain workers, nor heartsick handworkers, in a world in which all men would be living in equality of condition . . .'

Middle-class reaction to the industrial slum was not always connected with medievalism, nor even with Anglo-Catholicism. It found expression in the works of Henry George and H. M. Hyndman, both contemporary with Morris. George was an American economist (1839–97), whose chief work, *Progress and Poverty,* was published in 1880. In it he drew attention to 'a general feeling of disappointment ... of unrest and brooding revolution'. This led him to ask whether civilization was on the decline. His conclusion was that it had reached a critical period.

... and that unless a new start is made in the direction of social equality, the nineteenth century may to the future mark its climax. ... Everywhere is it evident that the tendency to inequality, which is the necessary result of material progress where land is monopolized, cannot go much further without carrying our civilization into that downward path.[1]

Like other political thinkers of the day he saw that political equality is apt to be meaningless when accompanied by vast inequalities of wealth. Unlike most others, however, before and since, he had an argument in favour of equality. Instead of wasting time on theology and philosophy, he explained that inequality is a cause of friction and that friction is a hindrance to improvement.

To compare society to a boat. Her progress through the water will not depend upon the exertion of her crew, but upon the exertion devoted to propelling her. This will be lessened by any expenditure of force required for bailing or any expenditure of force in fighting among themselves, or in pulling in different directions ...

Improvement becomes possible as men come together in peaceful association, and the wider and closer the association, the greater the possibilities of improvement. And as the wasteful expenditure of mental power in conflict becomes greater or less as the moral law which accords to each an equality of right is ignored or is recognized, equality (or justice) is the second essential of progress.

Thus association in equality is the law of progress. Association frees mental power for expenditure in improvement and equality (or justice, or freedom – for the terms here signify the same thing, the recognition of the moral law) prevents the dissipation of this power in fruitless struggles.[2]

1. *Progress and Poverty.* New York, 1889, p. 486.
2. ibid., pp. 456 –7.

There is some drivel here about moral law, but the argument does not depend upon it. He assumes that people feel entitled to equality – it does not matter why – and that progress is impossible until they are given what they want. There is something in this idea but his parable of the boat needs completion. Progress may result from all pulling together but direction depends on the man at the helm. His theory of equality leads at once to dictatorship.

Henry George's sovereign remedy was the common ownership of land – 'in nothing else is there the slightest hope' (ibid., p. 295). Here he differed from H. M. Hyndman (1842–1921), the Ulster journalist, whose *England for All*, published in 1881, derived mainly, without acknowledgement, from Karl Marx. The following passage is a fair sample of his work:

... For the first time in the history of mankind the whole earth is at our feet.... In our own country, which has led the way to the new stage of social development, all can see that the lot of the many is sad, whilst the few are rich and luxurious far beyond what is beneficial even to them. Our action in redress of these inequalities and better ordering of our affairs will guide and encourage the world. We, perhaps, alone among the peoples, can carry out with peace, order and contentment those changes which continental revolutionists have sought through anarchy and bloodshed. ... Now ... is the time ... for Englishmen ... to push aside the petty bickerings of factions or the degrading influence of mere selfish interests, to the end that by sympathy and fellow-feeling for their own and for others they may hold up a nobler ideal to mankind. Such an ideal is not unreal or impracticable. Not as yet of course can we hope to realize more than a portion of that for which we strive. But if only we are true to one another, and stand together in the fight, the brightness of the future is ours – the day before us and the night behind. So, when those who come after look back to these islands as we now look back to Athens or Palestine, they shall say 'This was glory – this true domination ; these men builded on eternal foundations their might, majesty, dominion and power.'[3]

Karl Marx called Hyndman 'self-satisfied and garrulous'

3. *England for All*. London, 1881, p. 193.

and we need not quarrel with that description. It was Hyndman, nevertheless, who formed the Democratic Federation in 1881. The author of this nonsense was also the founder of the National Socialist Party in 1916; a name of which more would be heard at a later date. In the earlier days, however, the emphasis was more on the idea of democracy; with socialism its inevitable corollary. This was the message of Edward Carpenter, who wrote *Towards Democracy* in 1883. This was the period when socialists began to appear in local government, encouraged by the Municipal Corporation Act of 1882. The middle-class theorists were on the march. They were not, however, unopposed. There were some who knew from the beginning where their arguments would lead; and chief among these was Herbert Spencer.

In *The Man Versus the State* (1884), Spencer distinguished clearly between 'the regime of status' and the 'regime of contract'. The Liberals, he saw, had inherited a tradition of abolishing restraints wherever possible, but this they abandoned after 1860, their measures revealing a new itch to interfere. The middle-class socialists were gaining an indirect influence over the party, and their aim was to confer direct benefits on the working-class, tending towards economic equality. To give people greater freedom should enable them to benefit themselves. To benefit them directly, by contrast, one must insist, first of all, on obedience. And Spencer saw that regulations marry each other and breed. Under the heading 'The Coming Slavery' he wrote as follows on this subject:

... There is that increasing need for administrative compulsion and restraints which results from the unforeseen evils and shortcomings or preceding compulsions and restraints. Moreover, every additional State-interference strengthens the tacit assumption that it is the duty of State to deal with all evils and secure all benefits. Increasing power of a growing organization is accompanied by decreasing power of the rest of the society to resist its further growth and control. The multiplication of careers opened by a developing bureaucracy tempts members of the classes regulated by it to favour its extension, as adding to the chances of safe and respectable places for their relatives. The people at large, led to look on benefits received through public agencies as gratis benefits, have their hopes continually excited by the prospects of more.

A spreading education, furthering the diffusion of pleasing errors rather than of stern truths, renders such hopes both stronger and more general. Worse still, such hopes are ministered to by candidates for public choice, to augment their chances of success; and leading statesmen, in pursuit of party ends, bid for popular favour by countenancing them. Getting repeated justifications from new laws harmonizing with their doctrines, political enthusiasts and unwise philanthropists push their agitations with growing confidence and success. Journalism, ever responsive to popular opinion, daily strengthens it by giving it voice; while counter-opinion, more and more discouraged, finds little utterance.

Thus influences of various kinds conspire to increase corporate action and decrease individual action. And the change is being on all sides aided by schemers, each of whom thinks only of his pet plan and not at all of the general re-organization which his plan, joined with others such, are working out. It is said that the French Revolution devoured its own children. Here, an analogous catastrophe seems not unlikely.

The numerous socialistic changes made by Act of Parliament, joined with the numerous others presently to be made, will by-and-by be all merged in State-socialism – swallowed in the vast wave which they have little by little raised.

'But why is this change described as "the coming slavery"?' is a question which many will still ask. The reply is simple. All socialism involves slavery.[4]

4. *The Man Versus the State*. London, 1892 (1st ed., 1884), p. 314.

3

INTERNAL CONTRADICTION

In his approach to sociology and politics, Herbert Spencer had one tremendous advantage over rival theorists. More than most of them, he knew what he was talking about. When he tried to define the proper limits of state interference he was speaking as a former engineer of the Birmingham and Gloucester Railway. When he wrote of Social Statics he did so as sub-editor of *The Economist*. In sociology, moreover, his views were influenced by John Morley, a statesman of long experience with whom he was closely associated. All this gives added weight to some two, at least, of his observations. First, he pointed out that the socialists of his day were quite exceptionally lacking in practical ability. Second, he doubted whether the information was yet available on which their sort of theory could be based. He called, in effect, for research as a needed preliminary to any sort of conclusion; and his own research extended to one field that the socialists ignored – that of psychology. Of that subject he knew enough, even in those early days, to see the basic fallacy in communism; and this is what he wrote:

... The communist shows us unmistakably that he thinks of the body politic as admitting of being shaped thus or thus at will; and the tacit implication of many Acts of Parliament is that aggregated men, twisted into this or that arrangement, will remain as intended.

It may indeed be said that, even irrespective of this erroneous conception of a society as a plastic mass instead of an organized body, facts forced on his attention hour by hour should make every one sceptical as to the success of this or that proposed way of changing a people's actions. Alike to the citizen and the legislator, home experiences daily supply proofs that the conduct of human beings baulks calculation. He has given up the thought of managing his wife and lets her manage him. Children on whom he has tried now reprimand, now punishment, now suasion, now reward, do not respond satisfactorily to any method; and no expostulations prevents their mother from treating them in ways he thinks mischievous. So, too, his dealings with his servants, whether by reasoning or by scolding, rarely succeed for long; the falling short of attention, or punctuality, or cleanliness, or sobriety, leads to constant changes. Yet, difficult as he finds it to deal with humanity in detail, he is confident of his ability to deal with embodied humanity. Citizens, not one thousandth of whom he knows, not one-hundredth of whom he ever saw, and the great mass of whom belong to classes having habits and modes of thought of which he has but dim notions, he feels sure will act in ways he foresees, and fulfil ends he wishes. Is that not a marvellous incongruity between premises and conclusion?

One might have expected that whether they observed the implication of these domestic failures, or whether they contemplated in every newspaper the indications of a social life too vast, too varied, too involved, to be even vaguely pictured in thought, men would have entered on the business of law-making with the greatest hesitation. Yet in this more than anything else do they show a confident readiness. Nowhere is there so astounding a contrast between the difficulty of the task and the unpreparedness of those who undertake it. Unquestionably among monstrous beliefs one of the most monstrous is that while for a simple handicraft, such as shoe-making, a long apprenticeship is needful, the sole thing which needs no apprenticeship is making a nation's laws.[1]

Spencer goes on to suggest that the legislator needs to have a basic knowledge of biology and psychology, of anthropology and history. Without it, the past belief in the divine right of kings will be surpassed in mischief by the current belief in the divine right of Parliament. 'The function of Liberalism in the past was that of putting a limit to the powers of kings. The function of true Liberalism in the future will be that of putting a limit to the powers of Parliament.'[2]

1. *The Man Versus the State*. London, 1884, p. 365.
2. ibid., p. 403.

Although Spencer probably wrote this in the year of Karl Marx's death and published it in the year of the procession (see p. 41) to Marx's grave, it might be difficult to prove that it was Marxism that he had in mind; for Marx, after all, had died in obscurity. But there is an otherwise uncanny precision in the contrast he draws between communist theory and human experience. Karl Marx's worldly failure was complete, his inexperience quite exceptional, and his practical ignorance of the masses no less remarkable than the hatred he felt for people he had never even met. With every conceivable handicap, Marx was arrogantly certain that people would act in ways that he could foresee and achieve the ends that he would approve.

Karl Marx (1818–83) is best understood as a Jew without a country, a professor without a university position and an author without a public. To take these points in order, Marx was of purely Jewish descent on either side, both his grandfathers being rabbis and his mother barely able to speak German. All that was German about Marx was his education at Bonn and Berlin, where he specialized in philosophy, economics and history. A revolutionary from an early age, he was denied the academic career for which he might have seemed destined. Graduating Ph.D. in 1841, he joined the Communist League in 1847, for which he published the *Communist Manifesto* of 1848. Expelled in turn from France, Germany, Belgium and Austria, he fled to London in 1849 and lived there until his death. Almost any Jew can be stateless, but Marx was peculiarly so, born of alien parents in a frontier region between Germany and France, educated in the Rhineland and in Prussia, a student at Berlin but a graduate of Jena, exiled by the age of twenty-five and resident in London from the age of thirty-two. Nor was this domicile chosen from any love of England or of anything but safety. He knew next to nothing of the English when he died, preferring to live among German exiles, talking German, thinking in German and for preference writing in German. He knew of the toiling masses only from blue books and parliamentary reports. We hear nothing of his travels among the

48

Lancashire cotton mills and as little of his talks with the London poor. There is no record of his visiting the coalmines, the docks or even a public-house. He was essentially homeless, offering no loyalty and accepting no responsibility. And with his scorn went hatred. He despised and loathed his rivals, quarrelled with his allies and condemned all sympathizers who deviated even by a little from the doctrine he held to be sacred. Karl Marx had no country. He was always, first and foremost, a Jew.

He was also an unemployed professor, a scholar in the German tradition with a first-rate brain, a vast depth of learning and considerable obscurity of thought. Of his intellect and scholarship there can be no doubt at all. He knew many languages and had read widely in many subjects. A very learned man indeed, he was admirably fitted for the life of a German university. Marx's complete absorption in his philosophy, history and economics was quite typical of the sort of professor he should by right have become. That mixture of scholarship, vagueness, poverty and practical inexperience would have graced a chair at Heidelberg or Bonn. But for the death in 1840 of Frederick William III of Prussia, but for the succession of Frederick William IV, a man of strictly orthodox views on religion, Marx might have had an academic career. Barred from this, however, as an atheist, he had no class to teach; no pupils from whom he might have learnt. There is a sense, of course, in which a professor lives apart from the world. But his duties, even in the mid-nineteenth century, involved some contact with other people. The most professorial of German professors would have examinations to set and research to direct, meetings to attend and appointments to keep. Sessions of Senate and Faculty might give him scope for eloquence or intrigue and he would find for himself the need to compromise, concede and persuade. Howbeit painfully and slowly, the professor comes to know something of administration and finance. But this was the practical knowledge which Marx was denied. All the experience he had was in his own home, where his failure was catastrophic for his wife and family. Of his children some died of slow starvation and two committed suicide. Retaining and increasing all his professional learning, he became more purely theoretical than even professors are allowed to be. Of the difficulties of organizing human society he knew practically nothing. There was in fact no human society – no province or city, no school or club – of which he could be said to have been a member. His whole life was bounded by the printed page.

Granted, however, that authorship was his life, he failed to make any impression on the reading public. He had a profound belief in his own genius but it was a belief which few others could be brought to share. How completely he assumed the role of a new Messiah is manifest from the way he lived. On the altar of his genius he sacrificed his own health and comfort, his children's lives, his wife's happiness and another man's career. Making little effort to earn his living, he sponged continually on others. Engels largely supported him out of what he could earn on the Manchester Stock Exchange and Marx accepted this help as no more than his due and too little for his needs. His faith in his own genius would seem to have been immovable. All the more painful, therefore, was his continued obscurity. His reputation as a theoretical revolutionary never spread in his lifetime beyond a narrow revolutionary circle. His articles in German had only the smallest circulation. His American articles were unsigned. In England he was virtually unknown, of little interest even to the police. *Das Kapital* brought him a few German admirers but was not even translated into English until after his death, volume I in 1887 and the other two volumes in 1907. The original edition occasioned only one short review in the English press, another (by Engels) being rejected by the *Fortnightly*. Later historians, recording the quarrels among these nineteenth-century revolutionaries, are apt to forget that these protagonists (whatever their later fame) were all then quite unknown. Marx was no more than a shabby refugee living in Soho or Hampstead and working daily at the British Museum; a seedy figure huddled over his books or shuffling home to his wife, his children and his unpaid bills. Marx was certainly as obscure as any, not so much criticized as ignored.

To point the contrast we should remember that his period (1850, say, to 1880) was one during which British literary men were influential as never before or since. The novels of Dickens and Kingsley were indirectly preaching social reform before Marx came to London. Thackeray had earned over £5,000 a year by authorship, and Anthony Trollope (1815–82) made as much or more, yet neither having quite the fame of Alfred Tennyson. It might be asked whether a Jewish author of foreign appearance could hope to do the same. But that was exactly what the novelist Benjamin Disraeli did. Drawing attention to social evils, Disraeli did far more than earn a living. Entering Parliament in 1837, he became Prime Minister in 1868, achieved an earldom in 1876 and died only two years before Marx himself. If Marx resented his poverty and his lack of success (and he clearly resented both), he had before his eyes the examples of men who equally saw and described the evils of industrialism, who attacked established abuses and who brought about actual reforms but who were nevertheless invited to the great houses where they moved almost as equals among the titled, the wealthy, the politically brilliant and famous.

Marx had some cause to be bitter, but his lack of success had another and more important result. He never encountered the criticism of men whose experience he was bound to respect. The professional author clashes privately with his publishers and agents, with people who think that his views as expressed are too extreme or too repetitive. He finds that editors are just as cowardly and obtuse and that sub-editors do their work without reason or wit. He clashes, finally, with the reviewers and with people he meets at the club. 'I don't accept your theory,' says the general, 'and I doubt whether you believe in it yourself.' People, he finds, can be maddeningly argumentative. Worse still, they can turn out to be right. Even when wrong, however, they provoke the author to find the retort that will crush them. In one way and another he comes to realize that opposition serves a purpose, and that his intellectual weapons can rust if he is for too long unopposed. Marx, by comparison, was the prophet on the mountain top. Into a single tremendous task he threw the concentrated energy of a lifetime. He brought to his work an immense learning, a complete selfishness, an impressive intellect and a fanatical devotion. Talking into the void, however, he heard no muttered 'Rubbish!' from the wind that blows on Sinai.

What was Karl Marx's message to mankind? It was enshrined, first of all, in the *Communist Manifesto* of 1848. In that he argued that the history of all hitherto-existing society is the history of class struggles. Last of these was the triumph of the bourgeois class over feudalism. The current struggle is between the bourgeoisie and the proletariat. The bourgeoisie has created modern industry for its own profit, but the tendency of this process is at once to impoverish the workers and drive them into alliance with each other. Once so allied, their object must be to overthrow the bourgeois supremacy and seize the industrial machinery for themselves, abolishing nationalism and private property in the process and making themselves the ruling class. Classes and class antagonism will then be abolished. The communists are those destined to lead the workers in their struggle and the workers must take no notice of those who profess any other form of socialism. Communists deplore these other varieties of socialism as calculated to lessen the antagonism between the classes and so postpone the conflict without which the bourgeoisie can never be overthrown. The communists will nevertheless support any revolutionary movement against the existing social order. Their aims cannot be achieved without violence. Let the ruling classes tremble! The proletarians have nothing to lose but their chains. Working men of all countries, unite!

The revolution which Marx sought to encourage was something he regarded as imminent in 1847. It was not a revolt against large-scale industry, for there was none at the time; least of all in Germany where his revolution was supposed to begin, or in France, where a revolution of sorts did actually occur. In so far as an industrial society existed it was in England. But the English factories, which Marx had not visited, were still in their infancy and there was nothing comparable anywhere else. His exhortation, therefore, to the world's proletariat was addressed to a mere handful of artisans in a mainly agricultural society. Such revolutionary activity as there was did no more than establish Napoleon III in France and Bismarck, eventually, in Germany. Marx came to realize that no revolution was imminent. More than that, *The Origin of Species* appeared in 1859 and may have suggested to him that evolution is a slow process. From about this time he began a systematic study of economics, hoping to find in this a key to the revolutionary process. He collected material from 1859 to 1865 and began to write his chief work in January 1866. It was finished in April 1867 and printed in August. This was *Das Kapital,* Vol. I, the work upon which his reputation mainly depends.

Das Kapital, Vol. I, runs to nearly 900 pages (perhaps 400,000 words) in the English version and is far from easy to read. It takes the form of a textbook of economic theory and cannot as such be regarded as anything but obsolete. His theory of value had its vogue at the time but has, of course, been superseded. There remains his Dialectical Materialism and his Theory of History. As a materialist, Marx believed that the only world is that which we perceive with our senses, and that our ideas are only a reflection of that world. Dialectical Materialism is the belief that evolution is a process of conflict, contradiction or struggle between two opposing forces or ideas, their mutual destruction producing a third idea which is different from both. Thus the result of the conflict between private property and the proletariat is the abolition of both property and class. Those who accept this theory believe that the violence of collision is essential if the desired result is to be gained. The belief that any compromise would be fatal might serve as an excuse for Marx's violence of language. The fact is, however, that his hysteria is partly social and partly the effect of his sedentary life. Powerful as a thinker, Marx was personally intolerant and spiteful, morose and treacherous, theoretical and quarrelsome, cowardly and vain.

When we come to consider Marx's theory of history, we have to remember that it dates from 1848, if not indeed from about 1841. He had thus formulated his conclusion before he even began to study the facts. That might be thought a serious criticism but his economic interpretation of history breaks down, in fact, at two other points. In the first place he refused to admit that any other interpretation is possible, his view being the only one. But the absurdity of that is obvious. That ideological and political ideas are influenced by material or economic circumstances we should mostly admit. That they are influenced by nothing else is a ridiculous oversimplification. In the second place, a theory of history must rest, like any other theory, on facts; and the required facts, in Marx's day, were simply not available. His was a theory of economic history based on one incomplete example. Knowing nothing of how the process would end, Marx had little opportunity of knowing how it had even begun. For the systematic study of history began after Marx's time. Cunningham's *Growth of English Industry and Commerce* did not appear until 1882, and our knowledge of economic history has progressed since then almost as dramatically as our knowledge of physics. Scholarship has thrust backwards into prehistory, forward into the events which have happened since Marx lived, outwards into Oriental and American fields hitherto unknown, and inwards into the history of science, of which we have barely scratched the surface. Whereas we have evidence of civilizations rising and falling over a period of at least 30,000 years, Marx rests his economic theory on an analysis of about 500 years of one civilization; an analysis formulated before the standard histories had even been written and leading to a conclusion which he had announced before his researches had even begun.

That a supposed textbook of economics should end as the bible of an Asian religion might have come as a surprise to the atheist who wrote it. But our concern is not with Marxism as a creed but with *Das Kapital* as an influence on socialism. It was to prove, in fact, very influential indeed. For while British socialists might reject 'the bible of the working man' as contrary to the methodism in which they had been brought up, and inconsistent with the liberalism in which they still believed, they did accept two Marxist ideas. They came to believe that all problems are economic problems. They learnt to assume that economic history must be written with a political purpose. So far as Europe is concerned, Marx's triumph was in substituting economic for political thought. 'We are all socialists now,' said Sir William Harcourt in 1889, but there is a sense in which all modern politicians are Marxists. If Mr Harold Wilson and Mr Edward Heath agree with each other about anything it is in supposing (quite wrongly) that their problems are primarily economic. Mr Wilson studied at Oxford and taught Economics at University College. Mr Heath studied at Oxford an imitation of the course pursued by Karl Marx at Bonn. The language used by each is virtually the same, even when their conclusions are different. All is to depend upon prices and incomes, upon bank rate, tariff and rate of exchange. In the days of Gladstone the same problems of finance took second place to problems of general policy and even of religion. Questions merely political are seldom nowadays the subject of debate.

That the current controversy over (say) Britain's possible entry into the Common Market should be an economic debate is due to Karl Marx's influence. The readers of *Das Kapital* are given to understand that the revolution must come. 'The centralization of the means of production and the socialization of labour reach a point where they prove incompatible with their capitalist husk. This bursts asunder. The knell of capitalist private property sounds. The expropriators are expropriated.' Up to this point Marx has many stirring things to say. He is the more plausible, moreover, in that he is, so far, an evolutionist. He describes not a static but a fluid situation, being concerned essentially with the laws of change. But evolution, for him, ceases on the day of proletarian triumph. As from that point he becomes a mere utopian or visionary. The proletariat, he explains, being in power and with no opponents left, would find politics so needless that the State would wither away. The abolition of army and church will be the preliminary, merely, to the abolition of everything else. As from this moment Marx has no further advice to give. Specific about all the institutions that are to be abolished, Marx has practically nothing to say about what is to take their place. He says something vaguely about a commune and about universal franchise, leaving his disciples to work out the details for themselves. But why should centuries of development end, as it were, with the blast of the whistle? If capitalism is to fail by reason of its internal contradictions, allowing the proletariat to set up a communist utopia, we can fairly ask what is to happen next. Why should communism not fail in its turn, giving place to dictatorship? What is specially permanent about that regime as opposed to any other? Evolution does not come to a standstill. Nor, if it did, should we know at what point it might be expected to stop. Why should the State wither away? Should we not rather suppose that the nationalization of every industry would give any government the cue to expand and ramify? Granted, however, that the Revolution is to represent finality, we should expect to hear more about the utopia which is to result. But Marx's political ideas end with the lamp-post on which the last capitalist is to be hanged. He loses interest at the point where our excitement should be feverish. If it is to paradise we are journeying, we hear nothing of its glories. If heaven lies ahead we glimpse nothing through the gate.

The clue to Marx's apparent stupidity lies in the period at which he lived. To a man born at Trier in 1818 the idea of modern industry was completely alien. Its development came mostly after his time, leaving him free to suppose that peasants could run factories for themselves. But where Marx was merely ignorant, of necessity, his followers lack the same excuse. They press on, with bloodshed, towards a golden future which they cannot even bother to describe. Like the Old Testament from which its style derives, *Das Kapital* is based upon revelation, not argument. Marx (like Isaiah) tells us what is going to happen. He does not explain how he comes to be so certain about it, nor why the change has to be regarded as progress. He is weakest of all in psychology, being convinced that capitalists are all inherently wicked and that workers are virtuous by definition. He cannot see that capitalists and workers are the same sort of people with the same sort of motives, the capitalist being the worker of yesterday and the worker the capitalist of tomorrow. He is far less realistic than Herbert Spencer, failing to see that the proletariat of his imagining is as fallible as the communist friends with whom he almost invariably quarrelled. As Herbert Spencer himself pointed out, it is the people who cannot manage their own affairs who feel most confident about ruling the world.

Socialists in Britain are usually eager to explain that their own party is the strongest defence against communism. Says Mr Harold Wilson on this subject:

There are those who believe that the assertion of public responsibility for the means of full employment, social advance, material or spiritual, is a fatal step in the direction of Communism. It is our belief that a socialist approach to Britain's problems so far from being a lurch in the direction of Communism means the fullest flowering of democracy.[3]

He goes on to claim that socialist success has almost eliminated communism in Britain, and that the Labour Party will show the way towards 'a more balanced, satisfied society in which human dignity is accepted as the ultimate aim of economic activity'. He maintains that a system based on unemployment and waste – the system favoured in the United States – must be unstable; so much so as to prove an actual handicap in the struggle against communism. 'It is our task', he concludes, 'to give a lead to the free world in resolving this internal contradiction.' To many these sentiments must seem admirable. To others they may seem vaguely unctuous and smug. But there is most significance, for our present purpose, in the actual choice of words. The object of socialist policy is to gain full employment and social advance. The aim

3. *The Relevance of British Socialism*. London, 1964, p. 108.

of economic activity is to uphold 'human dignity' (whatever that may mean). To Marxism he is utterly opposed, but he follows Marx in all that he omits. In the process of government – in the actual machine which is to advance along the road to utopia – Wilson shows no interest at all. Like Karl Marx he thinks it enough to throw in a word about democracy, as if that were enough to solve the problem. That the machine has broken down he does not even notice, such is his eagerness to point the way. And, last of all come the few words which say so little and yet reveal so much. 'It is our task to give a lead to the free world in resolving *this internal contradiction.*' The voice may be the voice of Harold Wilson. The words are those of Karl Marx.

4

TANGLED WEBB

WE have described some of the elements which went to form the British Labour Party. To the Puritan tradition was added the idea of progress. Comes next the Industrial Slum from which people sought to escape through methodism, through the Co-operative Movement and through the trade unions. The flight of those entrapped in the slum attracted the sympathy of middle-class intellectuals, who viewed the slum from outside. Some, like William Morris, were shocked by all that is hideous in industrialism. Others, like Hyndman, were shocked rather by the contrast between poverty and wealth. Socialism was the remedy they preached, their argument no more than a logical extension of the democracy in which liberals already believed. What is the use of political equality, they asked, in a world of economic serfdom? The socialists had no real philosophy of their own and no clear idea of what they were trying to do. Behind them, however, lurked a more formidable character. As compared with these wavering sentimentalists, Karl Marx was an intellectual giant. Although they borrowed his ideas, however, usually without acknowledgement, the socialists agreed to reject his leadership. They realized that his atheism would have weakened a movement already quite weak enough. There was something disconcerting, for that matter, in Marx's alternation between economics and hysteria. If people are really governed by immutable laws, why should Marx complain of their ruthless vandalism? If capitalists are motivated by 'the most infamous, the basest, and the most odious of passions', we must have moral criteria by which to judge them. But a code of behaviour can be nothing, after all, but a bourgeois anachronism, unacceptable to any materialist, and anathema to Marx. Uneasily aware of this dilemma, the British socialists found, eventually, a prophet of their own.

Considering these different elements, we must realize at the outset that they do not, of necessity, lead to the formation of a Labour Party. In other countries where the same elements exist, and notably in the United States, the result has been entirely different. The triumph in U.S.A. of the North over the South eliminated some elements which would have been anti-socialist. But the various forms of unrest were never unified. Attempts to form a federation of trade unions began in 1866 and were renewed in 1872, reaching a peak of success in 1885. A new attempt was made by the I.W.W. (Industrial Workers of the World) in 1905 but the movement, being pacifist, was suppressed as treasonable in 1917. The Co-operative movement made little progress until after World War I. When it began to succeed its most rapid progress was among farmers, whose Agricultural Co-operatives are now a colossal organization with a $17.2 billion turnover between them in 1961–2. These have little in common, however, with the trade unions and less with any attempt to form a Labour Party. As for the American intellectuals, they were mostly communist in the 1930s. They made pilgrimage to Russia and talked heatedly about the Spanish Civil War. Then communism was nationalized and their activities became more or less treasonable after World War II. Apart, however, from the inherent difficulties of the task, there was nobody in U.S.A. capable of merging these discordant elements into a coherent whole. In Britain, by contrast, this feat was performed, not indeed by one person but by three. The British Labour Party was the creation, essentially, of Beatrice and Sidney Webb and George Bernard Shaw. The brilliance of their achievement is seldom recognized, and cannot be assessed except as against the failure of others elsewhere and since. What no one could do in France or Spain, what no one even attempted in U.S.A., they did so effectively in Britain as to rule that country for fifty years. They did in the twentieth century what Jeremy Bentham did in the nineteenth. They provided Britain with a philosophy, a programme and a creed.

Beatrice Potter (1858–1943) was the daughter of a financier of Yorkshire and Puritan origin whose very intellectual wife died in 1882. Beatrice (aged 24) had moved in Gloucestershire and London society until then and now became a hostess in her own right. Tiring quickly of this existence, she began to visit the East End slums. Other ladies then did the same, but Beatrice Potter graduated from London to Lancashire, visiting the industrial region from which her mother's family had come. Among her Bacup relatives she learnt of the Co-operative Movement and its close association with methodism. She thought it offered an ideal training for local government – itself a useful defence, she thought, against the 'socialistic tendency of the coming democracy'. By 1884 she had decided to devote her life to sociological research. While Octavia Hill and Canon Barnett were labouring for the good of the poor, Beatrice (who knew these philanthropists well) preferred, like Charles Booth, to collect the facts upon which future policy should be based. She was sufficiently well known to give evidence in 1888 before the House of Lords Select Committee on Sweating. Moving among people who were concerned over social evils, she inevitably met members of the Fabian Society. According to George Bernard Shaw, she considered a number of these as possible husbands, inviting them in turn for weekends at her home near Gloucester. Her choice fell on Sidney Webb (1859–1947), a civil servant in the Colonial Office, and they became engaged in 1891. The marriage took place the following year, when her father's death left her with an independent income of £1,000 a year. Sidney Webb resigned from the Colonial Office, and they went to live at 41, Grosvenor Road. With F. W. Galton as his private secretary, Sidney began to campaign for election to the L.C.C.; a preliminary, it seemed, to his candidature for Parliament. He was already a known socialist, a man of lower-middle-class origin who had risen by competitive examination. Summing up the situation after their engagement, Beatrice wrote:

We are both of us second-rate minds, but we are curiously combined. I am the investigator and he the executant; between us we have a wide and varied experience of men and affairs. We have also an unearned salary. These are unique circumstances. A considerable work should result if we use our combined talents with deliberate and persistent purpose.[1]

They were childless, their first offspring being *The Co-operative Movement of Great Britain* by Beatrice Potter (1st ed. 1893) and its logical sequel *The History of Trade Unionism* by Sidney and Beatrice Webb (1894). It was the latter work which made them famous.

In observing that 'the firm of Webb' was unique in its assets, Beatrice was not overstating the case. Descended from nonconformists and liberals, it was her nonconformist conscience which drove her to the Lancashire factories and London slums. Unique already in knowing both (in contrast with Karl Marx who knew neither), she made herself the accepted authority on the Co-operative Movement. She then married a Fabian Civil Servant and candidate for the L.C.C. who helped her to become, with him, the accepted authority on the trade unions. In an exceptional way the Webbs thus united in themselves the elements which were to make the British Labour Party. More than that, they were aware of their opportunity in being uniquely acceptable to the housewives as consumers, the workmen as producers, the civil service as experts and the intellectuals as fellow theorists. His skill on committee was backed by her position in society, her aggressiveness tempered by his modesty. It was no accident that when he finally entered Parliament he was the only intellectual to represent a mining constituency. When they studied the intersecting circles which bounded the groups they could regard as progressive, they saw themselves as uniquely included in all of them. They covered between them the whole movement from the Co-operatives to the T.U.C., from local government to the civil service, from Toynbee Hall to the Methodist chapel, from Bernard Shaw to H. G. Wells. To crown the whole they had only to add (as they

1. Mary Agnes Hamilton, *Sidney and Beatrice Webb: a study in contemporary biography*. London, 1933.

chose to do) the London School of Economics and the *New Statesman*.

The London School of Economics dedicated to 'sociological investigation' was founded in 1895, occupying two small hired rooms in John Street, Adelphi. Its move from there to 10 Adelphi Terrace was financed by Mrs Bernard Shaw. When the University of London was reorganized by Haldane and Sidney Webb in 1899–1900, the London School of Economics was made one of its constituent colleges, with Webb himself as Professor (unpaid) of Public Administration. The objects of this institution were excellent, but its critics felt that the sociological evidence collected there was to prove the case for a socialism which was not so much defended as assumed. Future graduates and members of its teaching staff were to include Graham Wallas, L. T. Hobhouse, Sir William Beveridge, Clement Attlee, Harold Laski, Hugh Dalton, R. H. Tawney, Kingsley Martin and Sir Alexander Carr-Saunders. The *New Statesman* came much later in the Webbs' career, in 1913, and was originally financed by them, by Ernest (afterwards Lord) Simon, Edward Whitley, H. D. Harben and by George Bernard Shaw. It had, initially, a circulation of 2,500, which rose afterwards to 14,830 in 1931 and which stands now at about 90,000. The name chosen for this weekly was intended to emphasize the solid respectability of socialism. Clifford Sharp was the first editor, Desmond MacCarthy the dramatic critic and Shaw an expected contributor who seldom, in fact, contributed. The actual quality of its contents has fluctuated considerably, its tone being too often tiresome and querulous. It forms, nevertheless, part of the 'considerable work' which was to result, and did result, from the Webbs' partnership. The Labour Party as we know it is largely the work of their hands.

It is important to realize, nevertheless, that their achievement was partly accidental. Believing as they did in socialist planning, they would have been content to see this introduced by the Liberals; or even, for that matter, by the Conservatives. Well known from 1895, the Webbs made a reputation for

themselves as wire-pullers, with Haldane as 'a steadfast fel-
low-conspirator for the public good'. Close association with
R. B. Haldane over the University of London Bill brought
Sidney much into Liberal opposition circles. But when the
Liberals split over the Boer War, Sidney's friendship with
Haldane brought him into the Imperialist camp as represented by Asquith and Grey; thus gaining the hostility of
Harcourt, Morley and Lloyd George. Worse still was his association from 1900 with Rosebery and Balfour; with the right-
wing Liberals and indeed with the Conservatives. The main
result was to gain the distrust of the Radicals, like J. Ramsay
MacDonald, who began to undermine Sidney's position on
the L.C.C. Wrote Beatrice in her diary for 14 March 1903:

I have been pondering over the question whether I could have
done anything to stop the 'slump in Webbs' on the Progressive
side. Of course, our attention has been absorbed in getting hold of
forces in the enemy's camp, and our frequent coming and going
has excited suspicion in our own. They have not the wit to see
that, if a Government is in power with an overwhelming majority,
it is no use fighting it – at least not unless the other way has
proved unavailing.[2]

What these suspicions might be is fairly indicated by further extracts from the same ingenuous source:

Went into dinner with Winston Churchill . . .[3]

Our season ended with a brilliant little dinner here to meet
Mr Balfour. . . . I placed Charles Booth next to him – I doubt
from his manner whether he knew who Charles Booth was –
wondered perhaps that a Salvationist should be so agreeably un-
settled in his opinions! Bright talk with paradoxes and subtleties,
sentiments and allusions, with the personal note emphasised, is
what Mr Balfour likes – and what I tried to give him![4]

Whether she succeeded must be a matter for surmise. But
the Prime Minister had not the slightest interest – as she
soon discovered – in the economic and social problems by
which she was obsessed. All that her party-giving achieved
was a suspicion about her motives. Aware of this distrust, she

2. *Our Partnership*. London, 1948, p. 261.   3. ibid., p. 269.
4. 24 July, 1903. ibid., p. 270.

asked H. G. Wells to account for it. He explained fairly bluntly that Sidney's tactical skill was too obviously 'foxy' and that Beatrice herself was insufficiently radical. She thereupon decided against trying 'to run the show' for at least some years. The sequel is best told in her own words:

June 10 [*1905*]. – The Progressives have turned Sidney off the party committee.[5]
We have slipped into a sort of friendliness with Balfour.
He comes in to dinner whenever we ask him.
November 23rd. – Appointed to the Royal Commission on the Poor Law. . . . Yesterday evening we dined with Lord Lucas. . . . Mr Balfour was announced. . . . He was looking excited and fagged on the eve of resignation.
November 29th. – Yesterday A.J.B. lunched with us, and went afterwards to G.B.S.'s new play *Major Barbara*. The vanishing Prime Minister was looking particularly calm and happy . . . seemed like one with a load lifted off his mind.[6]

It is not the *resigning* Prime Minister with whom the rising politician likes to be seen. When Campbell Bannerman took office on December 5th his Cabinet included more talent than any formed since that date. With Grey and Asquith, Haldane and Morley, Lloyd George and Sydney Buxton – with Winston Churchill and Herbert Samuel among the Under-Secretaries – the government was one of extraordinary distinction. The Local Government Board was headed, however, by John Burns and not by Sidney Webb. In the Liberals' landslide victory, moreover, of January 1906, the 377 seats they gained included none for Sidney. Beatrice could busy herself with her Poor Law *Minority Report* in 1906–9, but the Webbs had lost touch by then with both Liberals and Conservatives. They had turned to the Labour movement, not solely from choice but as the result of failure in another direction. The whole history of British socialism would have been different had Sidney Webb been given office in 1905. He and Beatrice were forced, as it were, into the role for which they were so uniquely fitted.

The exclusion of Sidney Webb must have seemed a minor decision at the time. The major problem was to decide how far to the left the government should go. The trade unions, as we have seen (p.31), had gone into politics in 1900. Meeting in the Memorial Hall, Farringdon Street, London, on 27 February, their representatives had agreed to set up a Labour group in the House of Commons as distinct from the Liberals. Fifteen of their candidates stood, but Keir Hardie, at Merthyr Tydfil, was the only Labour member returned. There was better success in the election of 1906 but largely through a Lib-Lab alliance, and John Burns' acceptance of office seemed to give sanction to an arrangement by which Labour should pass, for the time being, as Liberal. This relationship was, in fact, precarious. The Liberal leaders had, therefore, two alternatives. They could stand by their principles and let the trade unions go their own way, or else they could adopt such Labour measures as would gain them trade union support. They tried, inevitably, to compromise, some inclining one way and some the other. They were uneasily aware that their original programme, the work of Jeremy Bentham, had been carried out. Their impetus had gone and with it the magic which once surrounded 'Peace, Retrenchment and Reform'. To stand against the socialists would be to lose what looked like a tidal wave of potential support. To adopt socialist policies would be ultimate suicide. The two alternatives were presented, respectively, by Asquith and Lloyd George. In October 1906, the latter told a Welsh audience that the Labour Party could sweep Liberalism away if the government failed to 'remove the national degradation of slums and widespread poverty', check 'the waste of our national resources in armaments' and 'tackle the landlords and the brewers and the peers, as they have faced the parsons'. A year later Asquith tried to explain at what point Liberals must make their stand against socialism. This is the point when liberty in its positive sense is threatned, as it must be, by a socialist reconstruction of society. Even he concluded, however, that 'the real danger lies in leaving evils unredressed and problems unsolved on the ground that, except by revolutionary expedients, it is beyond the competence of statesmen to deal with them'. The drift towards socialism had thus fairly begun.[7]

The turning point, Fred Jowett used to say, was a by-election in the Liberal stronghold of Huddersfield towards the end of 1906, when reports reached London that Mr Russell Williams, the I.L.P. candidate, was likely to win. This was the 'writing on the wall'. Mr Winston Churchill, then embarking on his Left Liberal phase, was sent post-haste to the constituency to announce the Government's intention to introduce Old Age Pensions. The Labour Party had won an important demand, but the Liberals won the election by the margin of 340 votes and regained the initiative. From this point onwards Mr Lloyd George dominated Liberal policy, cleverly manoeuvring Labour into a junior partnership in a half-hearted struggle against the House of Lords.[8]

While the Liberals were thus dragged, struggling, towards socialism, the Labour Party pulled further away from all that is liberal. In this move the leadership came not from the Webbs but from their close friend, Mr George Bernard Shaw. 'I am not a big man,' complained Sidney Webb at one moment of crisis, and the same thought occurred to him as early as 1894 when he admitted as much before the Fabian Society. 'Though we cannot count among our ranks any men of the calibre of Bentham and James Mill . . . I take it that the work set before us is analogous to theirs.' So indeed it was, but one may question whether the Fabian Society was as weak as he seems to imply. For if Webb was no genius, George Bernard Shaw certainly was. At least on the literary side the Fabians could boast of a giant. He had more influence over them, moreover, than they were always ready to admit. And whereas Webb would have taken office under the Liberals – had he been given the chance – Shaw was more ruthless in every way. An intellectual with little use for the proletariat,

7. S. Maccoby, *English Radicalism. The End*. London, 1961, p. 42.
8. Fenner Brockway, *Socialism over Sixty Years. The Life of Jowett of Bradford* (1864–1944). London, 1946, p. 78.

Shaw's approach was to the middle class; and it was Liberalism that stood in his way. Granted, moreover, that he was influenced by Webb, it is no less certain that Webb was influenced by him. That Webb was out of favour by 1905 was partly his own fault but partly the result of Shaw's persuasion. The process began with the publication, in November 1893, of the Fabian Society Manifesto. Under the title 'To your Tents, O Israel!' it appeared in the *Fortnightly Review,* signed jointly by Webb and Shaw, and was reprinted afterwards (1894) as a pamphlet entitled *A Plan of Campaign for Labour.* In it the joint authors attacked the right wing of the Liberal Party, alleging that its more enlightened members (Asquith, Acland, Rosebery, Ripon and Bryce) had been constantly opposed by the die-hards (Harcourt, Fowler and others) as also by 'the doctrinaire "Manchesterism" and pettish temper of Mr John Morley ... by the ignorance, indifference and inertia of the Whig peers, Lords Spencer and Kimberley, backed by such obsolescent politicians as Mr Shaw-Lefevre and Mr Arnold Morley.' The workers were urged, therefore, to form 'a Trade Union political Party of their own' with at least fifty candidates for Parliament. This they did soon afterwards, as we have seen, with results ultimately fatal to Liberalism.

It was the great tradition of the *Fortnightly,* founded by Anthony Trollope, that every contribution had to be signed, the editor accepting no responsibility for the contributor's views. In this instance there was a joint signature but all internal evidence points to Shaw as the actual author. The composition is characteristic, more especially where the literary style is allowed to influence the invective. The words chosen – 'ignorance, indifference and inertia' – were in the tradition of Jonathan Swift; an author to whom high office was always denied. Coming well enough from Shaw, who had no political ambitions, they were fatal to Sidney Webb. Were he to take office under the Liberals – and as late as 1904 he could see no other possibility – these pettish and obsolescent men would be his colleagues. They not unreasonably decided to do without him; a decision which was to have a significant sequel. But if Shaw was responsible for driving Webb into the Labour Party, he was equally responsible for steering the Fabian Society away from Marxism. Were we to adopt the Marxist terminology (which heaven forbid) we might conclude that Liberalism, the thesis, clashed with Marxism, the antithesis; their mutual destruction producing Socialism, the synthesis. It was Shaw who steered the Labour Party on its central course, avoiding the rocks on either hand. The aims of Liberalism had been mostly achieved by 1895, and Jeremy Bentham had no further message, silent as he was in his glass case at University College, London. Karl Marx had a new gospel to preach, one which involved a workers' rising against the middle class. In Lenin's hands this became a potent influence in the more backward countries, where peasants still formed the bulk of the population. It was wildly inapplicable to an industrialized country in which peasants and artisans would soon be hopelessly outnumbered by the bourgeoisie they were supposed to massacre. And while Shaw had a rather excessive veneration for Karl Marx, he had no poor opinion of himself. The doctrine he preached was essentially his own, therefore, and addressed to the middle class of which he was a member. Unfortunately for his legend, it was also addressed to a country in which Shaw chose to remain (like Marx) a foreigner; to people with whom he was never quite identified.

Shaw's platform was the Fabian Society, a group of left-wing intellectuals who came together in 1884. Elected to membership soon afterwards, Shaw joined the Executive Committee in January 1885. The Society's views were first announced in *Fabian Essays in Socialism,* published privately in 1889, the frontispiece by Walter Crane and the cover by May Morris. When 2,000 copies had been sold, it went into a shilling edition of 25,000 copies, with an American edition in 1894 and a sixpenny edition in 1908. It had, altogether, a considerable influence. These Essays marked the rejection of Marxism and the acceptance of a socialism which would be built upon existing institutions, existing society and the existing school of economic theory. Socialism is little more than the application of democratic principles to an industrial society. 'Socialism,' wrote Sidney Webb, 'is the economic side of the democratic ideal', and its aim can be achieved only by democratic means. And while Shaw advocated the formation of a Labour Party he never disdained the tactics of permeation. The Liberal Party was under socialist pressure from 1888, with social reform among its professed objects. The Conservatives' resistance was as feeble. And although it was 1923 before Webb announced 'the inevitability of gradualness', the infiltration was well advanced before he dared call attention to it. In the long run it was mainly the Conservatives who introduced socialism into Britain.

The socialism in which Shaw believed was implicit in most of his plays but is more explicit in *Major Barbara* (1905); the play in which he singles out poverty as the chief evil of the day.

... The universal regard for money is the one sound spot in our social conscience. Money is the most important thing in the world. It represents health, strength, honour, generosity and beauty as conspicuously and undeniably as the want of it represents illness, weakness, disgrace, meanness and ugliness.[9]

Brusquely discarding the Christian or charitable view of the subject, Shaw thought of the poor (and indeed the whole working class) as a public nuisance to be abolished. Whereas sentimentalists bewailed the fact that the poor were unhappy, Shaw thought they might well be as happy as drunkards or pigs. Making no secret of his dislike he explained that they were a source of infection and dirt and that 'mere poverty will not hurt them half as much as it will hurt their innocent neighbours'. The only remedy, he explained, is to pay everyone the same wage; not because that plan would be particularly fair but because the alternatives are impracticable, anarchical, impossible or absurd. He summed up his views on this subject in 1928, no better summary being published before or since.[10]

9. From the Preface.
10. cf. *The Intelligent Woman's Guide to Socialism and Capitalism.* London, 1928, pp. 19, 43, 95.

He explained at the same time that Hyndman and Morris had failed in their efforts to convert the working class – of which, for one thing, they knew too little.

... The Fabian Society succeeded because it addressed itself to its own class in order that it might set about doing the necessary brain work of planning Socialist organization for all classes, meanwhile accepting, instead of trying to supersede, the existing political organization which it intended to permeate with the Socialist conception of human society.

The existing form of working-class organization was Trade Unionism. Trade Unionism is not Socialism; it is the Capitalism of the Proletariat.[11]

Shaw's influence was considerable but mostly negative. He killed Marxism so far as Britain was concerned. He killed Liberalism as an intellectual force. He killed middle-class humanitarianism as applied to the poor. What was left after the massacre was the Labour Party as inspired by Beatrice and Sidney Webb.

Thrown aside by the Liberals, the Webbs had joined the Labour Party. Their moment of vision may have come in March, 1911, when Beatrice wrote as follows:

I am not sure that the time may not have arrived for a genuine Socialist Party with a completely worked-out philosophy and a very detailed programme.... I am not sure whether we had better not throw ourselves into constructing a party with a religion and an applied science.[12]

This, in effect, was what they did. The task was made the easier in that World War I prepared the way for socialism, Its potential opponents mostly died in action and the restrictions of wartime could be turned into the regimentations of peace. For the Labour leaders (many of them conscientious objectors) the war of 1914–18 was a period of planning. They were ready, therefore, when their opportunity came in 1924. By a fitting coincidence it was at the Webbs' house that the crucial decision was made.

11. ibid., p. 186.
12. *Our Partnership*. London, 1948, p. 471.

... From the start, Arthur Henderson urged acceptance of office. At a dinner in the Webbs' home, the six top leaders cast the die. Beatrice Webb noted: 'Sidney reports that they have all, except Henderson "cold feet" at the thought of office, though all of them believe that J.R.M. might not refuse.' Snowden's account agrees: Labour, it was felt, 'had no choice' but to accept office, despite all the hazards, for to do otherwise 'would obviously have been regarded as an act of cowardice'.[13]

13. Richard W. Lyman, *The First Labour Government*. London, 1957, p. 88.

5

THE FEET OF CLAY

THE Labour Party was an alliance, as we have seen, of trade unions, Co-operatives, Civil Service and progressively-minded intelligentsia. Its most obvious problem from the beginning was to reconcile the trade unions leaders with the Oxford economists; and to those outside the movement this must often have seemed the main weakness in the Party's structure. In point of fact the more serious defects in the alliance are due not to internal relationships but to the several weaknesses of each of the allies. Politically the voting strength of the Labour Party derives mainly from the trade unions, but in these we can also recognize the Party's central weakness. From the beginning the success of the trade unions was limited by the fact that each union existed to argue with the employer and thus depended upon the employer for its existence. Apart from that, however, there were other defects inherent from the beginning; defects which have become more obvious with the passage of the years and more obvious in time of triumph than they could ever have been in times of adversity.

To be understood, the Labour Trade Unions have to be studied in comparison with the Middle Class Trade Unions. If we seldom compare these different types of associations it is because we sometimes fail to recognize a trade union when we see it. The Bar Council or the Law Society may appear to be something different in kind. It is nevertheless the same situation, at different levels of society, that has produced the same result. Background to all this spontaneous association is the growth of a community in which individuals count for less and less. The move from the countryside to the market town and from there to the industrial city left the migrant with a sense of isolation and danger. In the villages from which people had come individuals counted for much even if families counted for more. With several generations simultaneously visible, the saying would go that those Browns were all daft, those Robinsons all mean. But there were characters too; the old soldier, the village atheist, the methodist grocer and the idiot boy. As people herded together in the centres of industry, the sense of family was weakened and the sense of individuality almost lost. Men became 'hands' in the factory and available 'labour' in the district. It would eventually become possible to talk of the 'masses' and the 'classes', either word suggesting a loss of individuality. To meet this new situation the obvious policy was to form organizations which would replace the family in its wider sense, at once protecting and absorbing the individual. Such organizations had always existed in the historic cities, more especially at the middle-class level. The migrant from the countryside, losing his rural identity, found a new status as member of a 'mystery' or guild. In this new capacity he formed part of a pressure group and friendly society, entitled to display his corporate insignia and sure at least of a well-attended funeral. These older organizations did not extend, however, to the new industrial areas, where the economic structure was, in any case, entirely different. Outside the ancient cities, and in London beyond the city boundaries, there grew up, during the nineteenth century, a new type of trade association. It was less local in character, being based more on the nature of the business than on the local patriotism of the parish. In its structure and purpose it could be either middle class or lower class.

The earliest middle-class organizations were the Church, the Bar, the Army and the Navy. At least the senior members of each profession could count as gentry, the most senior of all being in the House of Lords. Below their lordships the bishops and judges, the ennobled generals and admirals, the title of 'esquire' or 'gentleman' belonged of right to university Doctors, to barristers and to officers above a certain rank in the fighting services. At least some of these might expect knighthood. Beneficed clergy were gentlemen at least by courtesy, archdeacons and canons being gentlemen by right. Doctorates could be earned in Divinity, Law, Music or Medicine, and it was these which allowed the physicians to make their dubious entry. By calling themselves 'Doctors', even when merely M.B.s, they claimed (and still claim) the social rank which once went with a higher degree. The founding of the Royal College of Physicians (1518) marks the beginning of a campaign which had partially succeeded by about 1800; the year in which the surgeons began their own breakthrough. The pretensions of the other 'professional' bodies are at least symbolized by the sequence in which their associations were formed, as thus:

1768	Royal Academy.
1818	Institution of Civil Engineers.
1823	Royal Society of British Artists.
1825	The Law Society.
1831	Royal Institute of Painters in Water Colours.
1832	British Medical Association.
1834	Institute of British Architects ('Royal' 1887).
1844	Royal College of Veterinary Surgeons.
1847	Institution of Mechanical Engineers.
1868	Royal Institution of Chartered Surveyors.
1871	Institution of Electrical Engineers.
1879	Institute of Bankers.
1880	British Dental Association.
1880	Institute of Chartered Accountants.
1886	Chartered Auctioneers and Estate Agents.
1889	Institute of Journalists.
1889	Institution of Mining Engineers.
1891	Chartered Institute of Secretaries.
1897	Chartered Insurance Institute.
1899	Institute of British Decorators.
1901	Institute of British Photographers.

Claims to the professional status of 'gentleman' were thus advanced by artists, ships' officers, engineers, solicitors, architects, veterinary surgeons, surveyors, bankers, dentists, actors, stockbrokers, accountants, estate agents, journalists, secretaries and insurance agents. The claims would be followed by those of the almoners, shipbrokers, town planners, advertisers, chiropodists, travel agents and nuclear engineers. Nor need we suppose that the series has come to an end with the formation (in 1962) of the Institute of Legal Executives.

To what extent these claims are successful must be a matter of opinion. What is important, however, is that the claims have been made. Seekers of professional status have voluntarily limited the area of competition. Whereas the fishmonger might conceivably wish to drive all other fishmongers out of business, the dentist has accepted the idea that the other dentists are almost equally useful to the community. He joins with them in asserting the respectability of his calling and theirs, as also in barring from practice all those not properly qualified. Grocers or tailors may war with each other until half of them are bankrupt, but there is no comparable rivalry among chartered accountants or veterinary surgeons. It is against the interest of all to see the ruin of any one of them. The chartered accountant who should be reduced to selling matches in the street would bring a reflected disgrace on all the other chartered accountants. If it is desirable to the rest that the leading veterinary surgeon should be knighted, it is almost as important that the last of all should be kept out of jail. Members of the professions (whether or not they are recognized as such) are ambitious mainly for the class to which they aspire or for the class to which they belong. They may not be averse to entering heaven but they are more obviously intent on being regarded as gentlemen while on earth.

One might expect to find that the aim of these quasi-professional associations is to raise or maintain their members' income. The fact is, however, that their discussions centre more often upon entrance qualifications, educational programmes, examinations and prizes for excellence and current research into the arts or sciences with which they are concerned. With their interest in professional status goes a sense of responsibility towards the public and towards the pursuit of knowledge. Their journals are not political but technical, their conferences centre upon the latest ideas rather than upon the oldest grievances. With social aspirations – which may seem to some people absurd – go very definite ideals of conduct. Their weakness is in making a mystery of what is perhaps no more than a moderate skill, but the resulting sense of corporate pride has a value to the community. People who are intent on designing their associations' coat-of-arms will not spoil their public image by any minor dishonesties of practice. Still less will they lower their dignity by talk of a strike to gain higher fees. There are many actions which a professional etiquette must make impossible and these are broadly the deeds which seem ungentlemanly. The member of a professional association has a respect for the public and a still greater respect for himself.

Among the Labour Unions, by contrast, there is little talk of service to the community. The average trade union offers little more than a tried and traditional method of gaining higher wages by working for fewer hours; a method which depends upon the wage earners' unity of purpose. And while there may be something admirable in their loyalty to the movement and to each other, the workers' purpose remains at once material and drab. They do not rebel against industrialism as such. They do not demand work which satisfies their creative urge. They do not offer to take over the factory and run it at their own risk. They rarely ask so much as a share in its management. All that they have to suggest constructively is that the whole industry should be taken over by the State and that the State should be controlled by their own union officials. This demand, which is common but not invariable, implies that they want as voters to fix their own wages as workmen. This can only mean running the business at a loss, as must be normal in nationalized industries, and this is what many of them have realized. Some at least have grasped that the losses in nationalized industry must come out of the profits made by industries not yet nationalized. To nationalize all would not, therefore, be in the interest of those who are already on the public pay-roll. The drive towards nationalization falters, therefore, at this point, pursued doubtfully by those who feel (and rightly) that their immediate advantage might lie in joining the ranks of the state-employed; but that for all to do so would sink the boat into which they had climbed.

There is nothing discreditable in a man's desire to provide a better environment for his wife and children. But the unions were open to criticism from the outset and this for three reasons. They were and are unconstructive. They are and have always been aggressive. And they exemplify, finally, the failings of the giant organization as such. To bargain with employers about conditions and pay may be necessary, advisable or even heroic. It remains, however, a negative process: 'Concede this or we go on strike.' How negative it is we can deduce from the history of all the things they have failed to do. As compared with a medieval craft guild, the trade union has shown no interest in its particular trade. Members do not ask each other how their product can be improved, how their own firm can secure a lead over others, or how the industry as a whole can better serve the public and the world. While a craft guild was concerned with qualifications for membership, schemes of training, tests of competence and penalties for fraud, the unions have been merely intent on preventing the employment of non-members. Their interest has not been in the business or the product but in the wage levels applied to that or any comparable trade. Loyalty has often been intense but kept to the horizontal plane, a loyalty to workmates at the narrowest, to the working class at widest, but seldom to the work as such.

This is not to say that workmen have lost all sense of pride in what they do. The effect of industrialization is admittedly to weaken that sense, but pride still flourishes wherever there is room for it. Individuals retain some trace of the artist's egotism. They stand back when it is possible and say to themselves, 'That is a good job well done, neatly finished and made to last.' The craftsman's pride is thus as admirable as the soldier's honour or the poet's vision. But it is not through his union that this pride (where it exists) can find expression.

As compared with an ancient guild, therefore, the trade union remains colourless and empty. The medieval craftsman could say with a flourish, 'I am a Master Tanner. That is the Guildhall of my City Company. There is the banner we carry before us on festivals. There is the church we attend and this is the livery we wear. Here is our coat-of-arms, and that is the badge which even our servants can use. In time of siege we hold the city wall from the Barbican to the Mill Tower. Should I die, it is to the Tanners that my widow would look for aid. And, as I am childless, it is to the Tanners that my house will eventually be left.' The point about this declaration of loyalty is that the Craft Guild could arouse the sort of emotions which centre upon a public school, a Cambridge college, an historic regiment or a famous hospital. The boast 'I am a member of the Draper's Company' or 'I am a Fishmonger' comes incongruously from the retired colonel of today, but proves that the mystique is strong enough to survive the trade. And the sentiment has endowed the Guild with its hall and library, its pictures and tapestry, its banners and prizes, its scholarships and plate. The wealth of (say) the Cordwainers must derive from the fact that the more successful members retained their membership even after their business had come to be a matter of high finance. The guild survives, therefore, after the very word 'Cordwainer' has become meaningless. A cavalry regiment thus remains emotionally mounted even when mechanized, the idea being stronger than the fact.

The trade union's lack of appeal is not due to its lower-class origin (shared as that is with half the Livery Companies) but to its lack of external purpose. The Masons and Coopers had their own prosperity in view but that was never the sole object of their Guild. They were also concerned with their status, the reputation of their craft as compared with others, the fame of their city and parish, the distinction of their Aldermen and the stateliness of their Hall. As with any individual or family, what matters is the use to which surplus energy is put. In a public school, college or regiment, much effort goes into internal organization and welfare.

Reputation begins, however, at the point where that effort ends. The school will not be judged by its bedding and breakfast but by the fame or mediocrity of its pupils. The college's output is to be measured in terms of scholarship and research, not of sanitation and laundry. The regiment's reputation is earned not in barracks but in battle. The living and impressive tradition must always centre on the institution's external purpose. The ship is magnificent but only in relation to what she is doing or has done. She must be going somewhere, or must, at the least, have done something in her time. But this is where the Trade Union fails at the outset. It is a ship which exists solely for the benefit of its crew. It is not designed, like a cathedral, for the glory of God. It is not planned, like a palace, for enthroning a monarch. It is not organized, like a university, for the furtherance of learning. It was not raised, like a regiment, for the defence of the Realm. It exists for itself, for its members, and (perhaps) for the working class as a whole.

There is no crime in marching under a banner inscribed with the stirring motto, 'More pay, less work, better conditions and a closed shop.' The disadvantage lies only in the weakness of the army to which such a motto can appeal. Troops have often laid down their lives for God or the Emperor, for their regiment or for the Flag. You cannot expect them to lay down their lives in pursuit of a higher standard of living. For one thing, it makes no sense; the higher wages not being payable to those who have died in the effort to gain them. To endure discomfort with the object of securing eventual comfort is reasonable, but only up to a point. To perish, on the other hand, so that the next generation should be better paid is plainly absurd. And granted that a few people may sacrifice themselves in this or any other cause, all average common sense is against it. This being so, the union fails to surround itself with the glamour which is the attraction of the *Ark Royal*, the Black Watch or Fighter Command. It does not clothe itself with the outward show which suggests the inner meaning. It has no real equivalent for the Guards Chapel or the Royal Tournament. There is enough danger in mining to create a certain *esprit de corps*, enough to inspire a colliery brass band. But the unions remain otherwise colourless, incapable of attracting the bequests and endowments which go, by contrast, to the Freemasons or the National Trust. Some sentiment may attach to the singing of the lugubrious 'Red Flag'. There may be some talk about 'Martyrs in the Sacred Cause'. It is a question, however, whether the union's dependable support is equal to that which may surround a Third Division Football side. Lacking the quality of high romance, the members of a trade union have joined together for an object which is material at best and sordid at worst. There is a sense therefore in which their organization never quite comes alive.

That the trade unions are unconstructive has been apparent from their history. Demanding much that was reasonable, they have seldom claimed (as they might reasonably have done) a voice in management. Whether a concession in this field would have made for efficiency is perhaps doubtful. The point is, however, that the claim is rarely put forward. Employees seem happy to leave all responsibility to the management. Demanding, on occasion, that the management shall be nationalized, they admit from the outset that management must exist. This reluctance to assume any sort of responsibility is not the result of mere diffidence. The leaders' fear is that they may be identified with the directors rather than the men. They might be involved, moreover, in some labour-saving scheme which would reduce the numbers employed in a rival factory if not in their own. In a keenly competitive industry any one company may plan to drive another out of business. How can a director taken from the factory floor agree to that? His loyalty is not to the firm but to the wage-earners, to the men who may be thrown out of work. All this may be natural enough but the result is to confine the union leaders to a mainly negative task. If offered information, they would often rather go without it. If asked for their advice they have rarely anything to say.

If they are timid in some respects, the trade unions are aggressive in negotiation and cannot be otherwise. To keep in business a union has to do *something*. Each year there must be a fresh demand, without which the union will lose membership. Members expect to see some return for their subscriptions and union officials are not paid to be inactive. Lacking a grievance, they will have to invent one. Realizing this, the directors must make a show of reluctance, postponing the inevitable concession until it looks like a victory for the employees. If the union is quiescent it will lose membership, most probably to another union. Its officials, honorary or paid, can always gain consequence, on the other hand, from their decision to do battle. Any trade union has, therefore, a built-in aggressiveness, without which it can hardly survive. Nothing can be more damaging to the union official than the rumour that he is friendly with the management. This can only be the result of the blackest treachery, it is assumed, and the official has to stage a conflict in order to secure his own re-election. Aggressive towards management, the unions are almost as aggressive towards each other, competing for membership and staging frontier disputes over the exact territory which belongs to each. Nor is this perpetual unrest the fault of individuals. It is a characteristic of union organization and one for which there is no obvious remedy.

Unions have, finally, the urge to expand. To the extent that this expansion may eliminate inter-union conflict, this empire-building has its value. It also reflects the same tendency in management, the amalgamation of companies being paralleled by the amalgamation of unions, and may seem to that extent inevitable. But the organization which is the end product is not very different from the Industrial Group which is its natural opponent. The head office of the union looks very much like any other head office and has all the drawbacks which derive from complexity and size. For the aggrieved individual the union is almost as daunting as the Ministry of Labour, with just as great a likelihood of the file being lost or the matter being shelved. The union headquarters staff may run into hundreds. 'They are all working for *you*!' says the shop-steward to the newly-joined member. But this is manifest nonsense. They are working for themselves, for each other and for the organization, which exists again mainly for itself. As on the management side, moreover, the headquarters which is not merely rarefied and colourless is often ruled by a dictator; usually the man who planned the amalgamation in the first place.

The process by which a labour empire comes into existence is well illustrated in the story of the Transport and General Workers Union. Following the London Dock Strike of 1889 a number of 'general' unions came into existence under the leadership of Ben Tillett, John Burns, Tom Mann and Will Thorne. Tillett's springboard (formed in 1886) was the Tea Operatives and General Labourers' Union, with 300 members. After the successful dock strike this became, by amalgamation, the Dock, Wharf, Riverside and General Labourers' Union, with 30,000 members and Tillett as General Secretary. From London the movement spread to Liverpool, Bristol, Glasgow and Belfast. Between thirty and forty of these dockside unions were collected by Tom Mann into the Transport Workers' Federation. From Bristol, Ernest Bevin became assistant National Organizer of the Dockers. And when the final merger took place, fourteen organizations going to form the Transport and General Workers Union (in 1922), it was Bevin who became General Secretary. It was he who built Transport House, the union's headquarters in Smith Square, Westminster, which was also to house the Trades Union Congress. The T.U.C. was itself largely controlled by a working alliance between the Transport Workers, the Miners' Federation and the National Union of Railwaymen. Bevin's empire, at its height, comprised a huge membership, a fund running to millions, the *Daily Herald* newspaper and a virtual control of the T.U.C. The story of the National Union of Miners is broadly similar, one of its chief architects being Mr Arthur Horner. At the time of his retirement from the Secretaryship the Union had £170,000,000 invested in securities which ranged from denationalized steel shares to the freehold of the Café Royal.

By 1958 the giant unions numbered about twelve, the four

largest being the Transport and General, the Amalgamated Engineering, the Mineworkers and the General Municipal, all with over 775,000 members and the first with 1,266,000. Next in numbers came the Railwaymen, Shop Assistants, Civil Servants, Electricians, Teachers, Woodworkers, Public Employees and Post Office staff. Some smaller unions, as in the building industry, have formed a confederation for purposes of joint action. Other unions, small in themselves (as in printing), have a strong position in their control of some industry regarded as essential. The total number of subscribing union members is in the region of eight millions.[1] There are said to be about 3,000 full-time union officials, one paid organizer to about 2,700 members. Relatively few as they are, the officials are ill-paid, their salaries (in 1960) ranging from £750 to £1,250. The unions between them have a nominal capital of £84,000,000, equal to about £10 per head, much of it earmarked for provident purposes. Subscriptions have been kept low and the unions are notoriously bad employers; so bad that there has been at least one example of their office staff going on strike. Trade unions's premises remain unimpressive and shabby, their general atmosphere mean and drab. Theirs is a spiritless movement, at best.

When the tale has been told of what the trade unions have achieved, the even longer story remains of what they have never attempted. They have left no monument which anyone can admire. They have sponsored no art which their members could enjoy. They have made no contribution to industrial efficiency, invention or research. They came nearest to being creative when they owned and managed a newspaper. Its failure, however, was pathetic and the venture had to be saved (and was saved for a time) by Odham's Press. Experience had proved that trade union activities, faithfully reported, are seldom of the slightest interest to anyone outside the movement and make pretty dull reading for most of the people who are in. A favourite target for the Trade Union

1. See George Cyriax and Robert Oakeshott, *The Bargainers, A Survey of Modern Trade Unionism*. London, 1960, pp. 53–80.

critic is that wicked institution, the Public School. But there has never been anything to prevent a union financing a Boarding School of its own, one at which young members and future officials could be indoctrinated from the start. It could be more imaginative and adventurous than any school in the world. There has been nothing, save their own policy, to prevent trade unions from owning theatres and racehorses, cinemas, radio and television programmes. The T.U.C. could have founded its own College at Oxford, more exclusive than Christ Church and better than Ruskin. If the unions were dynamic and colourful there would be fifty ways of telling the public about their activities and ideals. The fact is however that there is nothing to tell.

Trade unions have not been concerned in anything creative but they *have* been concerned with power. As J. R. Clynes remarked:

An engine-driver rose to the rank of Colonial Secretary, a starveling clerk became Great Britain's Premier, the son of a Keighley weaver was created Chancellor of the Exchequer, one miner became Secretary for War and another Secretary of State for Scotland, while I, the mill-boy, reached the position of Lord Privy Seal, so that I might lead the House of Commons, and, later, become Home Secretary.[2]

Trade Union leaders have certainly reached positions of influence. Through most of their careers, however, there was the spirit of negation. Eager to lead their followers out of the slum, they have had no idea what to do next. To build up a wall of hostility between employer and employed is not particularly helpful when the need for the employer is tacitly recognized and where no plan exists for running the industry without him. The Trade Union is dull because it is unconstructive, tiresome because it is acrimonious, and ineffective (except politically) because it is too large.[3]

2. J. R. Clynes, *Memoirs* (1869–1924). London, 1937, p. 17.
3. The Co-operative Movement has not had the same political importance. Its later history is dealt with briefly, however, in Appendix A.

6

THE NEW SOCIAL ORDER

THE elements which went to make the Labour Party were knit together, and occasionally tangled together, by the Webbs. The result was a brand of socialism which the trade unions and Co-operatives were eventually made to accept. Beatrice Webb had seen the need for 'a religion and an applied science', both of which she could supply. Bernard Shaw saw to it that the religion should not be Marxism, nor Methodism (i.e. virtuous indignation) as it had been previously applied to politics. It was H. G. Wells who added the hint of scientific method. It was Sidney Webb, however, the methodical committee member, who translated faith and knowledge into a check list of things to be done. It was a work for which he was exceptionally qualified. The result was the detailed programme (see p. 71) of which Beatrice had first realized the need. Through it the Webbs were to govern Britain for the first half of the twentieth century. Up to a point indeed they govern it still.

Sidney Webb first outlined his programme in a lecture delivered to the Fabian Society in 1894. The Socialists' task, he explained, was to apply Collectivist principles to the actual problems of modern life; to those created by the Industrial Revolution. Given a highly industrialized country, with population massed round the factories, the choice lay between management by individuals and management by the community; for management there must be.

... To suppose that the industrial affairs of a complicated industrial state can be run without strict subordination and discipline, without obedience to orders, and without definite allowances for maintenance, is to dream, not of Socialism but of Anarchism.

... I do not urge the universal adoption by all Socialists of a rigid practical programme, complete in all its details. But our one hope of successful propaganda lies in the possession of exact knowledge and very clear ideas of what it is we want to teach ...[1]

As the result of further research and argument the principles of 1894 hardened into the more defined aims of 1901. In a lecture that year on *Twentieth Century Politics,* he called for a new policy of National Efficiency. This would involve a shorter working day, improved housing, higher wages, social security and a minimum standard of education for all. The aim should be an Efficiency 'by which every part of the central and local machinery of the State – not to say also the wider Commonwealth of the Empire – needs to be knit together into an organically working whole'.[2] It is characteristic of Webb, as indeed of Shaw, that the higher minimum wage is demanded 'not merely or even mainly for the comfort of the workers, but absolutely for the success of our industry in competition with the world'. Webb's teaching was effective and came to be embodied in the *War Aims of the Labour Movement,* drawn up and agreed in 1917. This led in turn to a more detailed manifesto, *Labour and the New Social Order,* drawn up by a committee of the National Executive. Edward Pease used to say that 'Whenever Webb is on a committee, it may be assumed, in default of positive evidence to the contrary, that the Report is his work.' In this instance the fact is sufficiently obvious; the Report is his. The capitalist system, he argues, has been largely destroyed by the war; and with it must go the political system in which it found expression. A new social order must take its place, based not on competition but cooperation, not on empire but on democracy; a social order characterized by 'a systematic approach towards a healthy equality of material circumstances for every person born into the world'. The 'Four Pillars of the House', based upon the democratic control of society, are as follows:

1. Sydney Webb, *The Basis and Policy of Socialism.* The Fabian Socialist, Series No. 4; London, 1908, pp. 70–3.
2. ibid., p. 83.

a) The Universal Enforcement of the National Minimum.
b) The Democratic Control of Industry.
c) The Revolution in National Finance.
d) The Surplus Wealth for the Common Good.

These, as explained, involve careful planning. It is the government's responsibility to find productive work for everyone, ending all risk of unemployment. It is the government's duty to provide better housing and better schools. It is for the government to reorganize railways and canals, forests and harbours; raise the school leaving age to sixteen and establish a 48-hour week. The democratic control of industry meant, initially, the democratic control of Parliament. There was thus to be adult suffrage equally for either sex with shorter parliaments and abolition of the House of Lords. There was also, however, to be a scientific reorganization of industry 'no longer deflected by individual profiteering, on the basis of the Common Ownership of the Means of Production'. This reorganization would involve the nationalization of land, of railways, mines and electricity plants; as also the steamship lines which would be absorbed into a National Service of Communication and Transport. Coal, of a uniform quality, should be sold by local authorities at a uniform price 'as unalterable as the penny postage-stamp'. As for finance, all indirect taxes (save on luxuries) would give place to direct taxation of private fortunes – with a capital levy to pay off the National Debt. In all this, it was claimed, the interests of the middle classes were 'identical with those of the artisan'. The Manifesto ends with this summary:

What the Labour Party stands for in all fields of life is, essentially, Democratic Co-operation: and Co-operation involves a common purpose which can be agreed to; a common plan which can be explained and discussed, and such a measure of success in the adaptation of means to ends as will ensure a common satisfaction. . . . [Whatever other people may do] no Labour Party can hope to maintain its position unless its proposals are, in fact, the outcome of all the best Political Science of its time; or to fulfil its purpose unless that science is continually wresting new fields from human ignorance. Hence, although the Purpose of the Labour Party must, by the law of its being, remain for all time unchanged, its Policy and its Programme will, we hope, undergo a perpetual development, as knowledge grows, and as new phases of the social problem present themselves in a continually finer adjustment of our measures to our ends. If Law is the Mother of Freedom, Science, to the Labour Party, must be the Parent of Law.

The content of this Manifesto was approved by the Party Conference on 26 June 1918. It was the programme offered to the electorate in December of that year. By 1922–3 Sidney Webb was Chairman of the National Executive Committee of the Labour Party, which gained 142 seats and polled 4,250,000 votes in the General Election of 1922. He himself became a Member of Parliament and, in 1924, President of the Board of Trade. Secretary of State for the Colonies from 1929, he entered the House of Lords in that year. As Lord Passfield he had great influence over the Labour Party until his death in 1947. It was he and his wife who had created the Party. Its political philosophy derived (and still derives) essentially from them. It is according to their ideas that Britain has been governed for fifty years. For much of that time the Labour Party has been out of office but the Conservatives have pursued the same policy, gaining lower-class votes on the understanding that they would do what the Socialists would have done if elected. Having lost the initiative, the Tories could only apply the brakes while heading in the same direction. In point of fact they have seldom even applied the brakes, such has been their anxiety to keep ahead of the electorate. This trick they had learnt from the Liberals, whose vote-catching Insurance Act of 1911 appalled the Webbs by its mere extravagance. 'Where,' asked Beatrice, 'are the professional champions of sound administration?' They were not among the Liberals and time was to show that they were not among the Conservatives either. 'We are all socialists now,' they told each other, and the pace they set was too hot at times even for their opponents. The march towards a socialist Britain began in 1905, its general direction being decided in 1894 and its specific aims laid down in 1917.

This being so, the early directives deserve careful study. What is apparent from the outset is that they involve two lines of thought. Socialism, we are told at the outset, is the economic side of the democratic ideal. All men are equal according to democratic theory but political equality is not enough. There must be 'a healthy equality of material circumstances', without which the freedom to vote is meaningless. Progressively-minded people are socialists, therefore, *because* they are democrats. Parallel to that line of argument is the case for Efficiency. A complicated industrial state requires strict subordination and discipline, a control extending to every part of the national life. From whence does authority emanate? Why, from the best political science of the day, for 'If Law is the Mother of Freedom, Science, to the Labour Party, must be the Parent of Law.' Where, finally, is the best political science to be found? Clearly, at the London School of Economics, as expounded by its Professor (unpaid) of Public Administration. Were the Webbs aware of this inconsistency? In a sense they were, but they taught themselves to believe that the Will of the People would point to the same conclusion as the voice of science. What if it did not? There can be no doubt that Efficiency, to them, was more important. But the democracy they were prepared to toss aside was the basic doctrine upon which their argument had been based. With that gone, the whole Fabian edifice had gone, including the demand for economic equality.

The choice just described between democracy and science is not fanciful. It was the choice presented to the Webbs when they visited Soviet Russia in 1932. They discovered that 'administrators in the Moscow Kremlin believe in their professed faith, and this professed faith is science'. They visited factories, farms and schools, Sidney whispering to Beatrice, 'See, see, it works, it works.' Here was a country where their dreams had come true. Russia was not, they admitted, a democracy; not at least in the accepted meaning of the word. But was that, after all, so important? Was not free thought and speech a mockery of human progress, wrote Beatrice, 'unless the common people are taught to think, and inspired to use this knowledge in the interests of their Common- wealth?'[3] Under Soviet Democracy people *had* been inspired to devote themselves to the public welfare. By this time the Webbs were virtually communist. It could be argued that their minds were failing, she having reached the age of 74 and he being only a year younger. But communism had been implicit in their thinking from the start. It is implicit, for that matter, in their Manifesto of 1917, which involved (see p. 88) 'a common purpose which can be agreed to; a com- mon plan which can be explained and discussed'. But there is no suggestion that the plan can be *reversed*. Far from that, the purpose of the Labour Party must, by the law of its being, remain (like the price of coal) for all time unchanged. The Webbs had come to realize that the only substitute for the profit motive is a religion; and that Marxism is the only reli- gion which would serve their purpose.

If the Webbs were Marxist in the end there is a very real sense in which they had been Marxist from the beginning. For they had always laid emphasis on economics, paying only lip service to politics. The Labour Party's Manifesto promises universal adult suffrage, more frequent elections and the abo- lition of the House of Lords. In all other respects the House of Commons was thought a sufficient instrument of progress. But the parliamentary rule in which the socialists professed to believe was manifestly doomed by all that they intended to do. The British party system may have no particular merit as a form of rule but its abolition implies a little thought as to what should take its place. To be effective, Parliament has required two or more parties, with alternate periods of oppo- sition and office. One might assume, at first reading, that the Manifesto of 1917 implied a survival of that system. Further study reveals the fact that the alternation is to stop. For one thing, the socialists mean to annihilate their opponents. The capitalists are to be taxed and expropriated out of existence. The Labour Party, moreover, 'claims the support of four-

3. *The Webbs and their Work*, ed. by Margaret Cole, London, 1949.

fifths of the whole nation'. With this measure of support, and the common people having been taught to think, the House of Commons would have only the one political party, the monopolists of wisdom, virtue (and office). Granted that the one-party legislature might be an improvement, we are at least justified in wanting to know more about it. Merely to announce the change is like decreeing that cricket shall be played, in future, with one team rather than two. Conceding that this could be a useful reform, we should still want some guidance as to how the revised game should be played. Would it still for that matter, be cricket? But Sidney Webb followed Karl Marx in dismissing all such questions as irrelevant. Is the House of Commons to 'wither away'? Is it the right body to deal with a largely nationalized economy? Is it the right body to deal with anything? On these points the Labour Party has never had any accepted doctrine. Its original pro-gramme, drafted by the future Lord Passfield, demanded little more than the abolition of the Peerage. So far as poli-tical problems go, the Labour Party ignored them from the start, Marxist in this more than in anything else.

A final point about Labour policy is that it was always parochial and selfish. Whigs and Tories had often rallied the people in a cause less narrowly their own; not merely to resist Napoleon but to defend the nation's honour, not only to support the Reform Bill but to save Constantinople from the Russians. The electoral issue which split the Liberals in 1906, giving the Labour Party its opportunity, was that of the Boer War. The debate centred upon imperial policy, on representative government, the treatment of recent immi-grants, the Jewish problem, the rights of the Negro popula-tion, and the dangers of adding a Chinese element to a situation already quite complex enough. In so far as the South African problems were insoluble then, they may seem insoluble now, but the Boer War put them into sharp focus and they are among the most fundamental questions we have still to answer. With the advent of the Labour Party a popu-lation which had debated the most grave issue of religion and morals, war and peace – a population which had argued over abolishing the Slave Trade and over the legal rights of the Confederate Navy, was invited to think of nothing but its own welfare. By the law of its being the Labour Party's purpose would be for all time unchanged; the purpose of demanding higher wages for less work in pleasanter surroundings. The purposes of men have sometimes been nobler than that.

Consider the situation which faced Britain when the century began. The expansion of Europe had lost its momentum and the Oriental world was just beginning its recovery. Britain stopped its overseas advance in 1904 and fell back on the defensive; physically against the German Navy and morally against world opinion over the Boer War. The crisis of western civilization came in 1905, the point being reached when World War I had become inevitable. What was Britain's part to be in this changing world? Should the British write off their scattered Empire and follow, with Hilaire Belloc, the Path to Rome? Should they do the exact opposite, renewing the faith which had inspired their mission? Ought they to follow Rudyard Kipling or take their cue from Oscar Wilde? London was in intellectual ferment at this time, open to new ideas of every kind. Looking back (with after-knowledge) on the Edwardian scene, one might long to interfere. The whole future of Britain (if any) hinged on the dreadnought battleship and the fatal negotiations proceeding between the French and British generals. The Empire had entered into its decline and fall. A word of warning given then might have saved a million lives and the Commonwealth itself for another generation. The decisions being taken were to have the most momentous consequences for the world. The stage was being set for a tragedy from which western civilization would never recover. The theme is Wagnerian and the German orchestra is about to play its diplomatic overture. The curtain will rise on a show which will (literally) bring the house down. At this instant Mr Sidney Webb appears backstage with a demand from the scene-shifters for a minimum basic wage. The demand may be reasonable but it comes as a ghastly irrelevance.

The main weakness of the Labour Party's programme lay in the utter selfishness of its drab parochialism. Until about 1905 the British had possessed a sense of mission. Their homeland was a base from which they crusaded, not always effectively, against cruelty and injustice, against famine and disease. By recent standards their colonial wars were almost incredibly humane. Their reforms at home were related, at least vaguely, to their mission overseas. Industrial prosperity was needed to support the Navy, and the Navy was needed to police the seas. A wider suffrage would give more people a share in the national purpose. A more perfect freedom would be an example to the world. Against this background look at the Labour Party again. Their demand was for a higher wage level, a nationalization of industry, a heavier taxation of their political opponents and all surplus wealth for their own constituents. They showed no interest in the political machinery by which the country would be governed. They showed no interest in Europe or the Commonwealth. They had no views on the great problems of colour and creed, of trade and war. They showed no more enthusiasm than did any other party for architecture, or art, for literature or music; and as individuals they showed, if anything, less. At the end of the Webbs' plea for Efficiency one is bound to ask 'Efficiency for what?' It is not enough to campaign for better houses and better health; these things are only means to some other end. The Labour Party was fortunate in having the guidance of Sidney Webb. It is less fortunate in having to share his limitations.

Where the Webbs were parochial, Bernard Shaw admittedly was not. The greatest author and dramatist of his day, he did much to enliven the Labour Party's drab image. He too was a puritan, however; nor was it he, for that matter, who wrote the Party's Manifesto. As compared with most of his critics he was of course an intellectual prodigy. Against one of these, however, he was fairly matched. This worthy opponent was G. K. Chesterton, catholic and liberal, thinker and poet. Attracted originally to socialism, Chesterton saw its weakness almost immediately. For Shaw, on the other hand, he had the warmest admiration and more especially for the way in which that great man had sacrificed so much for the cause in which he believed.

Here was a man who could have enjoyed art among the artists, who could have been the wittiest of the flaneurs; who could have made epigrams like diamonds and drunk music like wine. He has instead laboured in a mill of statistics and crammed his mind with all the most dreary and the most filthy details, so that he can argue on the spur of the moment about sewing-machines or sewage, about typhus fever or twopenny tubes . . .[4]

Chesterton went further than that in his generosity, meaning every word of it, but this praise was part of his argument. He admired in Shaw 'a passion so implacable and so pure'. In twenty years of debate he had read no reply from G.B.S. which was not fair minded and genial. 'It is necessary to disagree with him as much as I do, in order to admire him as much as I do; and I am proud of him as a foe even more than as a friend.' Time has underlined this point with an unexpected emphasis. For Shaw, with his knowledge and love of music, could have had success on a far bigger scale. Financially, his biggest rewards came from the two plays which were turned into musical comedy; *Arms and the Man* as *The Chocolate Soldier* and *Pygmalion* as the posthumous *My Fair Lady*. There was nothing, however, to have prevented Shaw from enjoying the latter success in his lifetime. He could, for that matter, have written it as a musical in the first place. As Chesterton points out, he could have 'drunk music like wine'. Rejecting the world of art Shaw turned to the Fabian Society, to the world of Beatrice and Sidney Webb. He stands almost alone among that group in having made (like Morris) a tremendous sacrifice on the altar of socialism. In his highly individual way, Shaw was a religious man 'implacable and pure'.

In discussing socialism G. K. Chesterton conceded at least one argument in its favour. Given a situation of real crisis, as might be found in the worst of the slums, something might have to be done at once. And the action taken – as in

4. G. K. Chesterton, *George Bernard Shaw*. London, 1911, p. 88.

fetching the fire-brigade or lifeboat – would be a collective responsibility. 'This is the primary and powerful argument of the Socialist and everything he adds to it weakens it.'[5] But life does not consist of emergencies. There has also to be a normal way of living; one in which the ordinary man gives expression to himself through his property and his work. As his industrial work becomes more tedious and mechanical his other means of expression – through his house and garden – become all the more important. Given ability and ambition he may desire greater scope for his individuality, a farm with woodlands or a place by the sea. Supposing he strives to this end, adding to his usefulness and working half the night, he may fairly want his son to inherit all that he has finally acquired. But the socialist warns him against being so selfish. He should be content to live like his neighbours, enjoying 'a healthy equality of material circumstances'. If he has greater inventiveness or energy it should be devoted to the common good. If he has children they should start on a level with the children next door. In the world of economic equality one man is as good as another and the rewards of each should be approximately the same. Considering this plan of life, G. K. Chesterton never made the conservative mistake of saying that it is impossible. He knew that it is feasible because monks have done it. They are unmarried, it is true, but celibacy may not be essential and the early Christians seem to have practised communism without it. What they did *not* attempt was living communally without *religion*. And Chesterton saw that this was the root of the matter. If we are to interfere with ambition, saying to the hard worker, 'Relax and live on your basic wage', we shall cripple our industry for lack of his assistance. That is not, therefore, our message. We are to appeal instead to his altruistic nature. 'Splendid!' we are to exclaim. 'Work after hours, by all means. Work all night and at the weekend – complete your new invention, develop your special skill. Do this, however, for the good of mankind. You must go without this property on which you have set your heart. Your reward must be in

5. ibid., p. 88.

the knowledge that you have served your fellow men.' In making this appeal we are asking more than the man of energy has to give. There are some – and both Jeremy Bentham and George Bernard Shaw might be counted among them – who will devote their lives to the service of man. Their number is negligible, however, beside the crowd who will devote themselves to the service of God. To exact the necessary sacrifice, socialism must be a religion. It must, in fact, be communism.

Chesterton emphasized the difference between early Christians and modern socialists. 'Elaborate a broad, noble and workable system', say the moderns, 'and submit it to the progressive intellect of society.' The early Christians preferred the direct approach, saying, 'Sell all that thou hast and give to the poor.' And Chesterton saw, as few others have done, that this advice goes to the heart of the matter. For the sacrifice we are asking people to make must imply a tremendous and lifelong demand on their patience, cheerfulness and good temper.

... Mere state systems could not bring about and still less sustain a reign of unselfishness, without a cheerful decision on the part of the members to forget selfishness even in little things, and for that most difficult and at the same time most personal decision Christ made provision and the modern theories make no provision at all.[6]

When challenged on the subject of their own incomes the socialists usually brush the inquiry aside. To accept a voluntary poverty now is not the same thing as to advocate that everyone should accept it in a hundred years' time. But how can one capitalist blame the others for setting no better example than he does himself. How can we recommend a poverty we are not even ready to share? Should we apply for admission to the Communist Party or the Society of Jesus, we must be prepared for immediate hardship and effort. It is not enough, we realize, to accept the desirability of sacrifice by someone else at some future time. It is not sufficient

6. G. K. Chesterton, *What's Wrong with the World*. London, 1912. p. 73. et seq.

to proclaim our belief in the inevitability of gradualness. For us at least, if not for others, the Kingdom of Christ or of Lenin must already have come. Our membership will be in an Order for which we must be ready to die. As compared with the Jesuit or communist, therefore, the socialist is a pitifully feeble character, a propagandist of abstract virtues which he does not even exemplify, pointing to a road which he does not even pursue.

We have seen that Beatrice and Sidney Webb lived as capitalists, talked socialism and ended in the communist camp. Bernard Shaw did much the same, reproving G. D. H. Cole on one occasion for claiming to be a Liberal Socialist: 'Now if Mr Cole is not a Communist he is not a Socialist.' For Shaw, as for the Webbs, experience and logic pointed to the same conclusion, that communism is a religion and that socialism is nothing. If the ablest people are to sacrifice nearly all that their skill may earn, accepting their new position with humility, patience and humour, the appeal to them must be in the name of God, and must come from somebody who has made the sacrifice himself. To what extent they may cooperate, and for how long, may be a matter of doubt. Nor does their cooperation leave us with all problems solved; for people denied the relatively innocent pleasures of possession can develop a far more insatiable appetite for power. If we allow, moreover, that power can ennoble (as it certainly can) we are still left with the need for faith. Our passion, like George Bernard Shaw's, must be implacable and pure. Suppose that it is, our strength being as the strength of ten, shall have to toss aside, however, is democratic equality. And we can go forth to conquer for Christ or Lenin. One thing we why not? Whoever heard of the Ten Commandments being put to the vote? Whoever saw a ballot box placed on the altar? If we hesitate now it is not from sentiment but from something half-remembered. Was it not upon human equality that our whole argument was originally based?

7

LEFT, RIGHT, LEFT

THANKS to the Webbs, the Labour Party came into existence, its strength based on the trade unions, its administrative experience improved on the L.C.C., its philosophy developed in the Fabian Society and its future leaders trained in the London School of Economics. Middle-class fears had been allayed by George Bernard Shaw, and Karl Marx was known to be the bugbear of H. G. Wells. Faced by this rising movement, the Liberals had tended to split, Lloyd George leading those who wanted to anticipate Labour demands. He was Britain's first democratic statesman; the first, that is, unqualified for office by birth, wealth, or education. He knew instinctively that socialism had to come. It might come, however, as he thought, in liberal guise; a gift to the working class from the party he aspired to lead. Had he known more about the trade unions he would have realized that a Liberal alliance was something they could not afford. For the union to survive it must triumph over opposition. Given a friendly relationship with liberal employers the union could not even exist. So the Labour Party's aggressiveness was vital to its political success. Its inevitable aim was to supersede the Liberal Party as the alternative to Conservatism.

What looks easy now, in retrospect, did not seem easy then. The Liberal Party was very much part of the British landscape, rooted in tradition and hallowed by achievement. If Lloyd George had ensured its eventual collapse, his actual presence gave promise of victory. As for Asquith and his other colleagues they were men of a quite astonishing distinction. To replace the Liberal Party might have taken fifty years of effort. Fate intervened, however, in the form of war. In 1914 the Liberals found themselves committed to a world conflict for which they were psychologically unprepared.

Their recent policy had centred more upon old-age pensions than upon battleships. They were more saddened than ex-cited by war, several ministers resigning at the outset and others are believed to have voted against it. Even in a Coalition Cabinet they mostly failed to impose their will on the admirals and generals. By its nature, meanwhile, the war made extraordinary demands on industry. Trade unions were in a position to make terms with government, and Labour's first great political triumph was in forcing Asquith to resign.[1] With Lloyd George as the wartime leader, the drift towards socialism was inevitably hastened. This involved the denial of all that Liberalism had ever meant. Instead of upholding freedom (with all the risks involved) Lloyd George's followers were now to prefer security, with all the centralized planning which must inevitably follow. Instead of concerning themselves with politics or religion, they were committing themselves to a programme of social reform. This weakened them in debate against those who really believed in it. And while the trade unions strengthened their position as against the wicked capitalist, the more theoretical socialists planned the utopia which was to be the result.

Quite apart from the Labour Party Manifesto, the war was itself a potent factor in the march towards socialism. While the theorists were demanding the nationalization of railways, the War Office had (at least temporarily) brought this about. And if the Labour Party's aims covered an improvement in housing, the Conservatives were agreeing to promise 'Homes fit for Heroes' as an encouragement to the troops. War and socialism go together in another way, for the wartime mood eliminates all thought of cost. Once it is agreed that the munitions must be produced, whatever the expense, it becomes easier to believe that houses and schools are as necessary and as free from financial considerations. There are moments, indeed, in time of war when the Conservative and Socialist come together in uneasy alliance. The Liberal, by contrast, must call in vain for 'Peace, Retrenchment and Reform'. He is the obvious loser and World War I brought

1. See S. Maccoby, *English Radicalism*. London, 1961, p. 199.

immediate consequence to the Tory general or magistrate. In the long run, however, the Conservatives were to lose heavily in prestige. Their generalship – as contrasted with the Liberals' diplomacy – was appallingly bad. Their future leaders mostly died amid the stutter of the machine guns, so many crumpled figures on the German wire. Worst of all, the war – or, rather, its aftermath – marked the decline of the British Empire. Conservative prestige was closely associated with imperialism, with the far-flung colonies, with the armed forces which could offer them protection, with the public schools which formed an essential part of the system. The moral strength of the Conservatives had always derived from the fact that the famine they were partly preventing in India was far worse than the malnutrition the Socialists were bewailing in Houndsditch. Of still earlier date was the Conservatives' reliance on Ireland. Blind in many directions, Karl Marx was oddly perceptive in this.

... I have come to the conclusion that the decisive blow against the English ruling classes ... cannot be delivered *in England* but *only in Ireland*.

Ireland is the bulwark of the English landed aristocracy. The exploitation of this country is not only one of the main sources of the aristocracy's material welfare; it is its greatest *moral* strength. It, in fact, represents *the domination of England over Ireland*. Ireland is therefore the great means by which the English aristocracy maintains *its domination in England* itself.[2]

Coming from someone completely outside English life, knowing practically nothing about the British aristocracy, that is a very penetrating remark. Its truth became apparent when Ireland was lost to the Empire in 1921. With the removal of the foundation stone the whole structure began to crumble.

On the subject of the Empire the Socialists had been deeply influenced by Marxist thought and more especially by *Imperialism*, a book written by J. A. Hobson and published in 1902. All colonies, according to Hobson, should be given

2. *Karl Marx and Frederick Engels on Britain*, Anon (ed.) Moscow, 1953, p. 504–5.

immediate independence; not so much for their own benefit as to prevent the wars of capitalist imperialism which would otherwise take place. By 1919 the Labour Party had incorporated this plan into its literature, qualifying its rejection of Empire by some rather vague references to the obligations which might possibly remain, as also to 'the moral claims upon us of the non-adult races'. But it was Hobson's choice which the Socialists preferred, as more damaging to the Conservatives than any continued 'trusteeship'. That a premature withdrawal might cost (say) a million lives does not seem to have worried them unduly. Knowledge of their proclaimed intentions had its effect, inevitably, on the colonial services. As time went on there emerged a new type of administrator, the specialist in conceding independence. Honours once reserved for those who had added new provinces to the Empire were now to be earned by giving them away; the highest commendation going to those who could do it faster than others had thought possible. In this atmosphere of tame surrender, with empire builders giving place to economic advisers, the Conservatives lost their sense of purpose. Their knowledge of the world was ceasing to have a political value. They produced no theorist of the same calibre as Sidney Webb, no author who could be fairly matched against George Bernard Shaw.

The end of World War I found the Labour Party in a potentially strong position. Their idea of a 'Party Image' derived from Graham Wallas, who invented that expression in 1908.[3] They had in J. Ramsay MacDonald what Beatrice Webb called 'a magnificent substitute for a leader', even if admittedly 'shoddy in character and intellect'.[4] They had won their battle over Trade Union political contributions by the Act of 1913, which made members contribute unless they expressly decided against it. They had the beginnings of a party organization with a head office staff quadrupled between 1914 and 1919. Henderson, who ran it, could recruit only the dreariest of paid staff but there was a wealth of

3. *Human Nature in Politics*. 1908, p. 84.
4. R. T. McKenzie, *British Political Parties*. London, 1955, p. 375.

energy provided by G. D. H. Cole, R. H. Tawney, Arthur Greenwood, Arnold Toynbee, as indeed by the Webbs themselves. Many authors of the day — Wells, Bennett, Carpenter, Havelock Ellis and Bertrand Russell — were more or less socialist. Even with all this talent, however, the Labour Party could gain only eleven seats in the General Election of 1918. They could note, however, that the triumphant Coalition included only 133 Liberals as opposed to 334 Conservatives. With Asquith, McKenna, Sir John Simon and Herbert Samuel unseated — and with Lloyd George under Tory control — the Liberals were falling behind in the race. They made, it is true, a final effort. Asquith was returned for Paisley in 1920 and had reunited the party by the time of the General Election in 1924. But the tide of opinion was against his party and the 159 members they returned were outnumbered by 192 members of the Labour Party. The numbers actually voting Liberal and Labour were about equal, but the battle was lost. As from 1924 the Labour Party provided the alternative to Conservatism. MacDonald's first period in office was brief and impotent, but the Red Scare which brought it to an end was even more fatal to the Liberals. As Bernard Shaw remarked, the Red Russian landslide 'enabled third-rate Conservatives to oust first-rate Liberals' — one result being 'a grave falling-off in the quality of the victorious party'.[5] The pattern of British politics has altered little since then.

With the virtual elimination of the Liberals, at least as serious candidates for office, Britain returned to a two-party system. Instead, however, of two parties divided on political issues there were two parties divided by economic interest. Karl Marx's class war had been almost brought about. But the old system of alternation was no longer possible. The Labour Party was committed, for one thing, to the destruction of its opponents. It was also apparent that socialist measures were mostly irrevocable. Industries nationalized could not easily be restored to private enterprise. Colonies given

5. *The Intelligent Woman's Guide to Socialism and Capitalism.* London, 1928, p. 221.

independence could not be brought again under imperial rule. Socialism was a one-way street so that the alternation of politicians saying 'Nationalize!' with politicians saying 'Don't nationalize!' would end with all industries nationalized. It was a general realization of this fact that did much to keep the Labour Party out of office for so many years. More important, however, was the technological trend of the twentieth century. A party called 'Labour' and based on trade unionists who regarded themselves as working class, a party with the cloth-cap image, must depend for its success on a proletarian majority. But the coal miners were dwindling in number and so were the textile operatives. Clerks and telephonists were multiplying, by contrast, and these regarded themselves as middle-class. The potentially nationalized railways and mines had been bankrupt in any case and the future lay with automobiles and with oil. The Labour Party was thus tied to a lower-class which was becoming obsolete. Much of its middle-class support came from the trade-unionized civil service, its members swelling from year to year.

The Labour Party's only experience of power between the wars came in 1929–31. It had no absolute majority even then, but it was able to carry out some of its own measures. Under MacDonald the party's strong man was Ernest Bevin, boss of the Transport and General Workers' Union, leader of the T.U.C., director of the *Daily Herald* and builder of Transport House. The other great Trade Unions were represented by Arthur Henderson, J. H. Thomas and J. R. Clynes. Herbert Morrison represented the London County Council and Sidney Webb represented the Fabian Society. Thus arrayed, they did something for housing, something for the miners, something for the unemployed and something for the colonies. They set up Marketing Boards and planned the London Passenger Transport Board. They raised the school-leaving age to fifteen and promised India the status of a Dominion. Towards nationalization of industries all that the Labour Government could do, with Liberal consent, was to pass the Coal Mines Act of 1930. This placed the industry under the control of a statutory body empowered to regulate prices and output. More might have been done but the year 1929 witnessed the beginning of the Great Crash. The collapse of the enterprises sponsored in Britain by Clarence Hatry sparked off the beginnings of panic on Wall Street. Markets rallied for a while but the market collapsed in October and the Great Depression had fairly begun. From U.S.A. it spread to Britain and Europe. During 1930 the situation worsened, and by June 1931 the Credit-Anstalt nearly had to cease payment. From Vienna the chain of disaster spread to Germany and seemed about to engulf the world. The governor of the Bank of England told the Prime Minister that money was short, that gold reserves were being exhausted and that no loan could easily be raised. Using this crisis, Ramsay MacDonald took the opportunity to resign, resuming office as head of a 'National' government with Baldwin as his Deputy. The Labour Party's second experience of office had been brought to an abrupt conclusion. In the General Election of 1935 the Conservatives – in virtual control since 1931 – won 459 seats, leaving the Liberals prostrate and the Labour Party disorganized and disheartened. There would be no other Labour Government until 1945.

The Socialists, it is manifest, had little opportunity for introducing socialism between the wars. As against that, however, the Conservatives' success in keeping them out of office depended on promoting the measures which the Labour Party would have introduced had it been in power. From socialist legislation introduced by Lloyd George the Houses of Parliament went on to socialist legislation introduced by Baldwin. There was no actual initiative on the Conservative side, merely a reluctance to go too far or too fast. So far as policy went, the accepted source of inspiration was the Fabian Society and the Left Book Club – the latter organized by Mr Victor Gollancz, with 50,000 members. There was thus the Rent Restriction Act of 1915, and the Employment Exchanges set up in the following year. The Whitley Councils for the stabilization of wages were set up in 1919. The

National Insurance Act of 1920 covered another 8,000,000 workers. The first step towards nationalizing the railways was taken in 1921 when the Companies were reduced to four. The Central Electricity Board was set up under the Act of 1926, the B.B.C. under the Act of 1927. The Local Government Act of 1929 was a first step towards nationalizing the hospitals. It was followed by the Poor Prisoners' Defence Act of 1930, the Public Health Act of 1936 and the Act of 1939 which created B.O.A.C. Nor was the story markedly different after World War II, the New Towns Act and Civil Aviation Act of 1946 and the Housing and National Parks Acts of 1949 were not reversed by the Conservatives who passed the Housing Repairs and Rent Act of 1954 and whose legislation set up the Marketing Boards of 1958. There followed the House Purchase and Housing Act of 1959 and the Charities Act of 1960. As for the Civil Service, its majestic rise in numbers from 282,420 in 1914 to 380,963 in 1920, and so to 575,274 in 1950 and 637,374 in 1960, was checked at one time by the Slump, but was never seriously affected by one government or another.

While socialism was still advancing, at least timidly, in Britain, democracy was everywhere on the decline. The dictatorships established in Russia and Poland (1918) were the pattern for those which followed elsewhere. Mussolini became Italian dictator in 1922, and other dictatorships were founded in this sequence: Spain (1923), Turkey (1923), Chile (1927), Greece (1928), Brazil (1930), Dominican Republic (1930), Argentine (1931), Guatemala (1931), Portugal (1932), Uruguay (1933), Austria (1933), Germany (1933) and Mexico (1934). It was no longer possible to speak of parliamentary rule as a goal for which all nations were heading. As from 1922 the common though not invariable pattern has been for democracy to turn into socialism, for socialism to end in chaos and for a dictatorship to restore some sort of order. Faced by this unnerving situation, the Labour Party found itself torn between its ideology and its pacifism. As recently as 1933 there were proposals for a General Strike in the event of the Government going to war. To what extent had the situation changed? Some socialists wanted to defend their creed and others decreed the use of force. And what, meanwhile, of the inevitability of gradualness? There seemed to be nothing inevitable about it. What, for that matter, of the concept of progress? That the world was improving was far from obvious. The crisis for the Labour Party came in 1935, following the Italian invasion of Abyssinia and Sir Samuel Hoare's talk of 'sanctions'. It was the year of the Fulham By-Election, when the least mention of war could apparently lose votes. Labour pacifists were led by George Lansbury. Another group, led by Sir Stafford Cripps and Aneurin Bevan, argued that armed force may be morally justifiable if deployed by a socialist government – all other force being imperialist, capitalist and wicked. Clement Attlee and Hugh Dalton were prepared to fight, if necessary, for collective security. Ernest Bevin swayed the Labour Party Conference by one powerful speech, and Lansbury left the platform, a broken man. Pacifism was (more or less) dead.

A second crisis followed over the Spanish Civil War; one typically described in these words:

Nobody alive today [1956] is going to get over 17th July 1936 – even the people who are young enough never to have heard much about it.

It was, as anyone can see by hindsight, one of the Great Divides of the Twentieth Century. It was, as some say, the day when the peaceful progressive Spanish democracy was attacked by the Fascist wolves . . .[6]

It may be questioned whether people do go around muttering to each other 'Remember the 17th July!' Much, after all, has happened since. But it was, we must admit, a bad year for socialism. With the rights and wrongs of the conflict we are not concerned. It is enough to observe that the socialists saw it in the terms just quoted. It was, to them, an attack by fascist wolves on a progressive democracy. What did they intend to do about it? Did they clamour for war? Did they plead for intervention? Did they intervene them-

6. *Tribune 21*, ed. Elizabeth Thomas. London, 1958. 'The Spanish Tragedy' by Claud Cockburn, p. 273.

selves? Socialism has been called 'A Faith to fight for'.[7] Did they fight for it? They did nothing of the kind. The cause called for devotion, for exultant self-sacrifice, for heroism. It was the battle, after all, between Right and Wrong. Meeting this challenge the socialists of Europe and America produced between them one International Brigade. It included the Sak-latvala or Attlee Battalion, visited by Mr Clement Attlee himself in December, 1937. With him were Miss Ellen Wil-kinson and Mr Philip Noel-Baker. Adding moral courage to their intellectual superiority, some 600 British idealists threw themselves into the fight. It was not a tremendous effort either in numbers or quality. The Labour Party could count, at this time, on perhaps 2,445,000 supporters and a pro-portion of these were actually unemployed. But none of the present leaders reached the firing-line and few of the intel-lectuals, save George Orwell, were to be seen there for long. W. H. Auden served briefly as a stretcher-bearer and his admirers found in the war an emotional but long-range ex-perience of which they wrote afterwards at considerable length. Visitors to the scene of conflict included Stephen Spender, Ernest Hemingway and Professor J. B. S. Haldane. Known sympathizers were the Duchess of Atholl, Mr J. B. Priestley, Mr Harry Pollitt, Mr R. H. S. Crossman, Mr Emmanuel Shinwell, Mr Victor Gollancz, Professor Laski and Mr H. G. Wells. Those who fought, by contrast, were prac-tically all communists. What Mr Mervyn Jones describes as 'The grand gesture of Socialist youth'[8] never took place. The heroes known to history begin with John Cornford (Tri-nity, Cambridge) and Felicia Browne (killed at the outset) and end with Mr Tom Wintringham (Balliol) and Mr Wal-ter Tapsell. Conspicuous among them were Mr Fred Cope-man and Mr Sam Wild, ex-sailors who had taken a leading part in the Invergordon Mutiny. As the British Communist Party numbered only 7000 at this time, the Attlee Battalion of 407 effectives when the war ended may be said to have done them credit. Of the socialists, only a handful supported

7. Title of book by Eric Deakins. Gollancz, London, 1964.
8. Conviction, ed. Norman Mackenzie. London, 1958, p. 198.

the Dependents Aid Committee, and in terms of military assistance their aid was of course negligible. That the Spanish Civil War was a crisis in world history one might fairly question. It was believed to be that at the time, however, and few among the British socialists thought otherwise. Theirs was not, however, a faith for which they were willing to die in battle.[9]

Feeble though their effort was, the socialists mostly abandoned pacifism in 1936. Their hatred, however, of fascism led some of them to support the idea of a 'Popular Front' with communists brought into alliance. A group led by Sir Stafford Cripps and including Harold Laski, Aneurin Bevan, John Strachey and Harry Pollitt, came out in favour of such a move. Ernest Bevin was appalled at the disloyalty of these 'rootless intellectuals' and set about having them expelled from the Labour Party. Their expulsion took place and was confirmed at the Whitsuntide Conference of 1939. The delinquents were restored to favour during World War II but the incident served to define the limits of socialism as then conceived. The Labour Party, standing 'For Socialism and Peace', opposed to fascism and no longer pacifist, was almost equally opposed to communism. That the one side was wrong did not prove that the other side was right. The logic of this was incontestable but the policy which resulted was somewhat unrealistic, leaving Britain eventually without allies of any kind. It was not, however, in foreign policy that the Labour Party was mainly interested. Since the depression began in 1930 their chief obsession was with unemployment. It remains to see what this problem was and what the Labour Party had to say about it.

Unemployment as a major problem dated from 1920, first affecting the coal industry. Cotton suffered next and shipbuilding suffered worst of all. After the Crash in 1930 the numbers of unemployed passed the total of two million. There were still a million out of work when World War II began.

9. Hugh Thomas, *The Spanish Civil War*. Eyre & Spottiswoode, London, 1961. See pp. 240, 376, 389, 392, 505, 508, 559 and 623. See also Bill Rust, *Britons in Spain*. London, 1939.

For this extraordinary state of affairs the responsibility rested upon the Government, the Trade Unions and the men themselves. That the Government should have 'done something' is now very generally believed. But the Trade Unions, in upholding the theoretical wage-levels, had their share in causing the depression; and the men, by refusing to move elsewhere, were also in part to blame. What is important, however, is that the record of the Conservative and Labour governments is not significantly different. Where they contrasted was more in their attitude to the Dole than in their efforts to create employment. It was under a Conservative government that Ellen Wilkinson organized the march in 1936 of the Jarrow unemployed, but it was under the same government that something was eventually done. Previous failure to take any sort of action may have been criminal but it is a crime for which MacDonald must share the guilt of Baldwin and Chamberlain. It cannot be claimed that the Labour Party had any real remedy to propose. Nor could they look for inspiration to their original aims and objects; still less, it might seem, to Beatrice and Sidney Webb. Faced by unemployment the socialist mind was blank.

The irony of the situation lies in the fact that the Conservatives and Socialists might equally have cured unemployment by being true to their own principles. We realize now, having learnt with blood, sweat and tears, that the right time to resist injustice is at the beginning. As each opportunity passes the task becomes more difficult, each year adding to the material and moral strength of the other side. In the situation which faced Britain between the wars the Japanese invasion of Manchuria (1931) was the first step in a sequence which would lead to World War II. Adolf Hitler became Chancellor of Germany in 1933 and Italy attacked Abyssinia in 1935. Hitler's march into the Rhineland (1936) gave Britain and France the perfect occasion for a war which would have halted the whole drift towards disaster. At that time, however, the Labour Party had not even ceased to oppose Rearmament; many of its own supporters being involved, indeed, in the Peace Pledge Union of 1934. As from that time things moved swiftly. Once the alliance had been made between Germany, Italy and Japan, Hitler went on to annex Austria and Czechoslovakia, making a general war inevitable in 1939. Against this background the defeat of the socialists in Spain was hardly noticed. But the irony remains that the marchers from Jarrow in 1936 were still talking of peace. In their own interests and ours their banner should have read 're-arm!'

This is an instance of all ideological, military and economic arguments leading to the same conclusion. The unemployed riveters of Jarrow might have been building the destroyers of which we were so soon to have such desperate need. This is not to say that rearmament is the only cure or even the best cure for unemployment. In this case, however, the calls of honour, prudence and compassion were one and the same. All that we needed was courage, a belief in the Empire or even a belief in socialism. And this was where our thought was bankrupt. The Webbs had laid down a programme (see p. 88) based on ideas of democratic equality and involving a minimum wage, the democratic control of industry, a revolution in national finance and an allocation of surplus wealth for the common good. Confronted by unemployment at home and mounting dangers abroad, the leaders of the Labour Party could find nothing helpful in their original brief. Their meagre stock of ideas proved irrelevant, there being (for one thing) no surplus wealth to distribute. But the worst gap of all in their pitiful programme was on the political side. Following the Webbs' every limitation, they paid practically no attention to the machinery of government. All questions were to be regarded as economic and they could never see that political decisions must always matter more.

The point the socialists had missed is that the political system is basic to whatever we plan. It is our means at once of scrutiny and transport. If the machine is out of action we can neither see our route nor follow it. As the century has progressed, Parliament and Cabinet have become steadily less efficient, their clumsy machinery creaking and groaning, their obsolete processes all wildly inappropriate to the actual scene. The central problem, we are told, is concerned with the balance of payments or the speed of inflation. But even if such problems were central – which they are not – we should still need the right tools with which to equip ourselves at the outset. Talk of democratic equality is futile, especially as coming from people who end as communists. What we need, first of all, is a machine that works. All we can say of the machine we have is that it is twenty-seven years since it nearly killed the lot of us and that nothing has been done to improve it since. The completeness of its failure is something of which people need to be reminded. When Britain declared war in 1939 the Fabian Society had done its worst. Seldom has a country been so manifestly unprepared for what was obviously going to happen. Sheer ineptitude reached its peak when Britain, without an ally in the world, and at war with Germany, was actually preparing to fight Russia as well.

Having escaped destruction in World War II – but without, heaven knows, escaping damage – our first task is to avoid running such a risk again. We were led to the brink of extermination by politicians who desired popularity and electoral success; by the fatuous, feckless and feeble; by men who cared nothing, it would seem, for the land they so nearly ruined. The system, which brought them to power by overwhelming majorities, is the system in which we apparently believe. This trust in the House of Commons is now an accepted article of faith, being enshrined in Fabian Tract No. 70, otherwise entitled the *Report on Fabian Policy*:

When the House of Commons is freed from the veto of the House of Lords and thrown open to candidates from all classes by an effective system of Payment of Representatives and a more rational method of election, the British parliamentary system will be, in the opinion of the Fabian society, a first rate practical instrument of democratic government.[10]

Whatever the opinion of the Fabian Society may be, the

10. Alexander Grey, *The Socialist Tradition, Moses to Lenin*. London, 1946. (Quote from Fabian Tract No. 70.)

House of Commons has nearly proved a first-rate instrument for national suicide. Nor has the Labour Party any plan for political reform. It is perfectly content, it would seem, with things as they are.

8

LEFT LUGGAGE

THE conclusion of World War II left Britain appallingly impoverished and weakened. This second world conflict had taken place before the country had even superficially recovered from the first. The casualties were lighter in 1939–45, due to better leadership, but they were damagingly selective. The best were killed of a generation bred from the earlier survivors. Politically, the feeble government of the pre-war years had discredited not only the political parties but the party system itself. Almost as disastrous had been the wartime propaganda. Instead of people being told that they were fighting merely for survival, they were assured, as in World War I, that they were fighting to make a better world for themselves and for their children. There was, of course, no conceivable chance of the world being improved in any way. How could it be? When was any society ever improved by destruction and bloodshed? In earlier wars, it is true, vast territories had been conquered at relatively little cost. But the British had this time nothing to gain and much to lose. As they fought to escape annihilation their Empire disintegrated under American pressure. For them more especially the final result of the war could not be other than disastrous.

Even the gloomiest situation can offer, sometimes, a ray of hope. Britain could, at that moment, have assumed the leadership of Europe. British military reputation stood at its highest and there was no rival power in the field. The opportunity was sensed, moreover, by Britain's wartime leader. He was ready to carry out what should have been the most astonishing feat in our national history. Here was a country which had devoted three hundred years to a campaign of imperial conquest. Aloof from the continent, the British had defeated their rivals and emerged in 1815 as the leaders of

European expansion. Winston Churchill was old enough to have fought at the Battle of Omdurman, old enough to be classed as a builder of Empire. It was for him to convince his countrymen in 1945 that the Empire had been lost and that Britain had now become, whether we liked it or not, a part of Europe. He had to explain that the chance which offered might never recur. Here was a Europe with Germany divided and crushed, with France and Italy reduced to impotence, with Spain and Austria amounting to nothing. It was for the British to forget everything they had learnt and assume a new part in a drama for which they had never rehearsed. They had to forget everything creative in their previous centuries of effort. They were to forget overnight their knowledge of Hindi, Swahili and Hokkien. They were to learn German or die in the attempt. Seizing their chance they might have taken the throne of the Holy Roman Empire. The whole history of the twentieth century hinged on this moment of decision.

What is astonishing, in retrospect, is how nearly the feat was performed. One might have thought that people brought up on Rudyard Kipling would not turn, overnight, to Hilaire Belloc. One could hardly expect that people whose houses were adorned with Chinese scrolls and Jamaican curios would suddenly appear in the Opera House at Vienna. It was not the retired colonels, however, who caused the difficulty. To a quite astounding degree they were ready to accept the situation in so far as they understood it. Regiments shifted to Minden or Munster could discover, to their surprise, that not all their history had been in Madras or Mandalay. The Alps are a possible substitute for the Himalayas. Where the opposition lay was in the Labour Party. Lukewarm as they might be about the Empire, the socialists were handicapped from the outset in their approach to Europe. Theirs was a party in which nationalization had the most narrowly national of purposes. Their contacts even with European socialists had always been minimal. In relation, moreover, to other countries, they were hampered by their own attitudes of political or puritan disapproval. They could not flirt with the

Russians without being suspected of treason. In Spain their friends had been defeated and in Portugal they had not even fought. Across central Europe the words 'National' and 'Socialist' had come to have unfortunate associations. As for the French and Italians they were always Catholic or atheist, dreaming meanwhile about their imperial past. The atmosphere of the Labour Party, as assembled at Blackpool, was not one in which many Europeans would feel at home. The General Election of 1945 was final, therefore, as far as Britain's foreign policy was concerned. The moment passed, leaving the British outside the European community, alone with their crumbling remnants of Empire. They had, as was soon apparent, some problems of their own.

Technically, the war years had transformed the industrial countries of the world. The most immediate problem was presented by the motor industry which had flooded the world with vehicles for which there was no room; a process which killed the life of the city before going on to kill the life of the countryside as well. A second problem was created by the aircraft industry, which was now preparing the world for the Age of Tourism. A third problem was presented by photography in all its forms, from advertising to television, giving the few an apparently irresistible influence over the many. Medical progress was a problem in itself, multiplying people beyond the space or food supply available. Automation in industry was creating a new science of management, removing the whole process still further from the sphere of 'democratic control'. Rapid developments in science were unaccompanied, however, by progress in political thought, so that belief in 'Progress' was on the wane. Crime, especially among juveniles, was on the increase and gambling had become a major industry. The one wartime shortage which became permanent was that of newsprint, the press never recovering its pre-war importance save as an advertising medium. Motion pictures had lost much of their popularity but paperback publishing was about to boom. In these and a hundred other ways the scene had been transformed since the days of Beatrice and Sidney Webb. It remained to see how the Labour

Party would react to the new situation. Conservatives were not under the same compulsion to react at all, but their instinct was to forestall the socialist demands. They brought in Sir William Beveridge to elaborate a new scheme of social security, based on obsolete calculations which turned out to be wildly incorrect. They supported Mr R. A. Butler in passing the Education Act of 1944. They tried, in general, to show that they could be just as socialistic as the Labour Party. They felt, and with some reason, that time was on their side.

What was the Labour Party's reaction? The central fact about the socialists of this period is that the Webbs had no successor. Although he was alive, admittedly, until 1947, Sidney Webb's own message dated from 1894 and there was no one able to modernize it. When Jeremy Bentham ruled mid-Victorian Britain he did it through a pupil, John Stuart Mill. The Webbs had no disciple of that calibre, let alone an active son. And such as they had – like R. H. Tawney – were apt to end as they did; that is, as communists, logically unassailable but politically dead. Given no fresh inspiration, the Labour Party clung to the doctrines it already had. Reaching for their grubby lecture notes, scribbled at the pre-war London School of Economics, the second-generation socialists went into action. They produced, between them, the Labour Party's Manifesto of April, 1945. Under the inspiring title *Let us Face the Future,* its authors planned to solve the problems of the past. Basic to their programme was the statement that 'The Labour Party is a Socialist Party – its ultimate purpose at home is a Socialist Commonwealth – free, democratic, efficient, progressive, public-spirited – its material resources organized in the service of the people.' Socialism, however, 'cannot come overnight'. The immediate plans are limited, therefore, to the nationalization of fuel and power, iron and steel, railways and road transport. 'The Bank of England is to be brought under public ownership.' There is to be public 'supervision' (not prevention) of monopolies, a maintenance of price controls and a 'programme' (not otherwise too fully described) for the export trade. What was significant about this was that it could all have been written – and far more lucidly – by Sidney Webb. Unrelated to the actual problems of 1945, the Manifesto is practically the same as appeared (see p. 87) in 1917, complete with the inevitability of gradualness. There is admittedly no mention this time of steamships, still less of airlines, but vague references to 'basic industries ripe for public ownership' as contrasted with 'big industries not yet ripe for public ownership' left the voter to assume that ripeness is all. In point of fact the industries first nationalized were not merely ripe but rotten. Be that as it may, the Manifesto was adopted at the Annual Conference. It was further illustrated, in discussion, by Mr Denis Healey who concluded that

the crucial principle of our foreign policy should be to protect, assist, encourage and aid in every way that socialist revolution wherever it appears.... The upper classes in every country are selfish, depraved, dissolute and decadent. These upper classes look to the British Army and the British people to protect them. ... We must see that that does not happen.

Such an operation was not particularly probable even then, but now that the Army – under Mr Healey's supervision – has been practically abolished, it is no longer even possible.

On the basis of this Manifesto the Labour Party won the General Election of 1945. The socialist vote numbered 12,008,512, the anti-socialist vote came to 11,942,632; a difference of 65,880. This gave the Labour Party 399 seats as against 213 for the Conservatives and 28 for Liberal and independent members.[1] There can be no doubt that much of the voting was *against* the pre-war Conservatives, as shown for example in the Socialists' capture of Birmingham (once the Chamberlain stronghold). Apart from that, it was time for a change. After fourteen years in office, the Conservatives deserved to take their turn on the opposition benches. They confronted a government led by Mr Clement Attlee and comprising among others Mr Ernest Bevin, Mr Herbert Morrison, Mr Hugh Dalton, Mr Arthur Greenwood and Sir

1. R. B. McCallum and Alison Readman, *The British General Election of 1945*. Oxford, 1947, p. 248. (See also Appendix I.)

Stafford Cripps. All these had been in office, and Mr Attlee, unlike most of his colleagues, had been in the army during World War I. The Labour members included 43 public school men and no less than six Etonians – Dalton being one of them. Trade Union representatives made up the stolid right wing of the party, tending to be far older than their Conservative opponents. Red revolution might be the talk among some junior ministers, but the leaders were too elderly for that, their ages ranging from 57 to 64. If there was an extremist among them it was Aneurin Bevan, the Minister of Health, and even he left an estate of over £30,000.

It was with an air of sober triumph that the Labour Ministers took office. Background to their mood were the memories of unemployment, the dole and the means test, malnutrition and the Jarrow march. They could be vindictive without losing public support, for the war had brought with it an increased interest in socialism. An almost worldwide movement to the Left, away from fascism, had done much for socialism in U.S.A., France, Belgium, Holland, Scandinavia, Australia and New Zealand. The principle of fair shares for all had been widely accepted, so much so that opposition was minimal. As John Connell has put it, 'There were no barricades to storm. The defenders of wealth and privilege turned out to be as orderly, as submissive, as eager for reform and progress as first-year students at the London School of Economics. Socialism came by consent.'[2] All this gave the Labour Party the confidence to rule. What it lacked was any hint of gaiety.

This was and is a traditional defect of the radical reformist element in our society, traceable to Puritan and Roundhead origins, a graceless consciousness of Grace, intellectual ability and moral emotional fervour devoid of wit or elegance. They were on the whole a sad and priggish administration. Attlee himself had a frosty humour when he chose to show it. Bevin, Morrison and Shinwell had the robust and earthy and likeable qualities of their various backgrounds. But Cripps or Bevan, or Dalton with

2. John Connell, *Death on the Left. The Moral Decline of the Labour Party*. London, 1958, pp. 45–8.

his booming laugh and his joyless grin? John Strachey and Edith Summerskill making the Ministry of Food into a perpetual dreary Thursday in a bad private school in wartime? And that array of humourless younger men – Gaitskell, Harold Wilson, Marquand, Mayhew, Foot, Wyatt – all as solemnly prefectorial as priggish? There is no glitter, no drama, and precious little fun, in the recollection of their years of rule. But of the moral impetus which they possessed in that period there can be no doubt at all.[3]

Moral impetus they had but no single idea of later date than about 1894. It was their mission to accomplish what the Labour Party had begun before MacDonald's betrayal. It was their creed to believe everything that Sidney and Beatrice Webb had believed. They had come thus to share the limitations of their oracle. Nor were they going to find any fresh inspiration in the Trade Unions or the Co-operative Movements. The Unions were working for their own ends and had become so many bureaucracies in which the salaried executive had taken the place of the demagogue. The same trend was manifest in the Co-operative Societies where the managers had become as middle-class as their rivals in private enterprise. The whole trend of the day was against the 'cloth cap' lower-classes, as Charles Booth had observed as early as 1902. It was presently apparent that $1/2$ per cent of the working-class were becoming middle-class each year. Of the working population 30 per cent would be on salary by 1951, 34 per cent by 1959. Many of these former wage-earners would have voted Liberal, given the opportunity, and a fair proportion would actually vote Conservative. If the Labour Party was losing its appeal for the new middle-class, it had, if anything, less appeal still for the young. Nothing is more significant than the fall in Labour support among younger voters. As for the Party's League of Youth, it was an ignominious disaster from the start. 'Its primary function', said the National Executive, 'is to foster interest among young people in the policy of the Party.' The young were never invited to influ-

3. ibid., op. cit., p. 52.

ence that policy or even discuss it. Whether their opinion would have been of value must remain a matter of doubt, but they might certainly have been happier if allowed their say. The League's history is one of a spiritless organization drooping under adult patronage. It was sufficiently defiant on one occasion to get itself disbanded, but it has more often presented a picture of drab ineptitude. The Labour Party has considerable appeal for the old and the sick, the retired and the pensioned. With the young, by contrast, its failure has been complete.

What did Mr Attlee's government achieve? Its general policy has been described as follows by Mr R. H. S. Crossman:

.. so far as overall planning is concerned, all the Attlee Government did was to retain the cumbersome system of war-time controls and apply it – not unsuccessfully – to the increase of exports, the prevention of post-war collapse of agriculture, the stimulation of private investment and the maintenance of full employment. Inevitably, as the war receded into the past, these wartime controls became more and more unpopular; even worse, they became more and more irrelevant as wartime shortages disappeared and the terms of trade unexpectedly improved. Already by 1950 the Attlee Government was uncertain whether to liberalise the economy or to substitute a new system of Socialist peacetime planning for the war economy it had taken over in 1945.[4]

But what happened in the meanwhile? Still following the old formula, the Labour government nationalized the Bank of England, the Cable and Wireless services and many of the internal and European Airlines. Followed the Coal Industry Nationalization Act (1946), the Electricity Act (1947), the Transport Act (1947), the Gas Act (1947) and the Iron and Steel Act (1949). All this was sufficiently uninspired and the welfare measures which followed the National Insurance Act (1946) and the Housing Acts (1946 and 1949) were not especially controversial. In a different category was the National Health Service Act (1946), which achieved a dubious

4. *Labour in the Affluent Society.* Fabian Tract 325, 1960, p. 8.

result with the maximum of friction, and the Representation of the People Act (1948) which abolished the university vote. In other respects Labour policy centred upon high taxation, full employment and strict control. Overseas the dismantling of the Empire led to the independence of India, Pakistan, Ceylon and Burma; all done with a total disregard of the consequences. By 1949 the Labour Party had no single idea left, and it was at this moment that George Orwell published his book called *1984*. This is a landmark as expressing the author's impatience with socialist complacency. For fifty years and more the Labour Party leaders had believed in the inevitability of progress. Their Social Democracy was bound to come and was certain to bring universal happiness. Readers of *1984* were suddenly made to realize that there is nothing inevitable about it. Socialism might not come at all and might prove – even should it come – a nightmare of injustice, oppression and cruelty. Orwell, who had actually fought in Spain, was left with no illusion about Progress. He could see, as could few other critics, that democracy was on the decline and that socialism, without democracy, means the end of freedom.

The General Election of 1950 revealed the Labour Party as a spent force. Its passion for social justice was irrelevant to the great issues of the day, which were never put to the electorate at all. Some 13,266,592 votes were cast for the Labour Party as compared with 12,502,567 for the Conservatives, 2,621,548 for the Liberals and 91,684 for Communists. In Parliament the Labour Party had 315 seats as against the Conservatives 298 and the Liberals 9.[5] With this greatly reduced majority the Labour Government continued in office until October 1951. Its fall was preceded by the resignation of its extremists, Mr Aneurin Bevan, Mr Harold Wilson and Mr John Freeman, who objected to the reduction in social expenditure in the budget. All that the Labour Party had to propose by this time was the 'examination' of the chemical industry and the setting up of a development council for shipping. Writes Peter Townsend of this period:

5. H. G. Nicholas, *The British General Election of 1950*. London, 1951.

No one knew what to assault. Instead of realizing that their work was only beginning, the Labour Party leaders thought it was at an end. They seemed to be drained of initiative by the effort of legislating. They no longer believed in any tangible social aim and had increasingly lost touch with ordinary people, These were the two frightening facts at the start of the 1950's. . . . Those who had discussed the plans for a new society so ardently during and immediately after the war found their hopes sadly deflated.[6]

By 1949 the aims of the Labour Party had been expressed in a pamphlet entitled *Labour Believes in Britain*. This contained proposals for the nationalization of industrial insurance, the cement industry, the manufacture of sugar, the distribution of meat and the supply of water. It tailed away finally in vague banalities about 'effective partnership' between government and industry. But what partnership was possible with a government still theoretically committed to the total nationalization of the means of production? Another manifesto, *Keeping Left* (1950), said little about further nationalization, or indeed about anything else. *Let Us Win Through Together* (1950) had little to add to the resounding appeal of its title. Caution seemed to be the watchword. While it might be true however that the Labour leaders *did* little, the threat was implicit in what they continued to *say*. It was manifest, moreover, that their extremists were becoming restive. One of these, Mr D. N. Pritt, summarized the position as follows:

WHAT IS TO BE DONE

. . . One cannot march towards socialism under the present leadership of the Labour Party. Nor can the battle be fought otherwise than by the strength of the organised working class . . . which . . . continues to hold the majority of the workers despite disappointments, betrayals and defeat [What is needed is a unity of the Labour Party, the working class, youth, intelligentsia and Communist Party]. We shall then have a struggle . . . to transform the Labour movement and the whole political atmosphere of the country. The struggle will succeed; we shall be on our way . . .[7]

6. *Conviction*, ed. Norman Mackenzie. London, 1958, p. 96.
7. D. N. Pritt, *The Labour Government 1945–51*. London, 1963, p. 458.

On their way towards *what*? All that the earlier reformers had wanted was to find a remedy for social evils. This had been very largely accomplished by 1950, when the number of people below the poverty line had fallen to 1.6 per cent of the total population as compared with 18 per cent in 1936.[8] It was now apparent to many that the path indicated by Mr D. M. Pritt could lead only to communism and that any other left-wing path led to nothing. The Labour Movement had reached stalemate and this lack of ideas was reflected in the results of the General Election of 1951. The Conservatives gained 321 seats as against the 295 held by the Labour Party and the 6 which remained to the Liberals. The socialists went into opposition and had the leisure to think afresh. What exactly were they trying to do? It was obvious, first of all, that the general trend was now against them, not merely in Britain but in many other countries of the world. Inflation rather than unemployment was the chief economic danger; and inflation was associated with left-wing politics. Abroad, the nearest potential opponent was communist Russia. At home, the socialists had become identified with heavy taxation, austerity and rationing. George Bernard Shaw's aim of abolishing the lower classes had been partly achieved. As for the nationalization of some basic industries this made little difference, it would seem, to their efficiency, contentedness or success.

Sidney Webb, Lord Passfield, had died in 1947; Beatrice in 1943. George Bernard Shaw died in 1950 and so did Harold Laski. R. H. Tawney's last essays came out under the title of *The Attack* in 1953. There was no further inspiration to be had from the major or minor prophets. As for the politicians, the best of the earlier leaders were either retired or dead. The most intellectual of them, Sir Stafford Cripps, had resigned, a sick man, in 1950, and died in 1952. Ernest Bevin, perhaps the ablest, died in 1951. There remained Clement Attlee, the party leader, capable but colourless; and

8. B. Seebohm Rowntree and G. R. Lavers, *Poverty and the Welfare State*. London, 1951. (The two surveys of 1936 and 1950 took place in York, taken as an average city from this point of view.)

Hugh Gaitskell, the party's official economist, a good chairman but no genius. What the party needed was another Sidney Webb and a fresh directive. All that it had was Aneurin Bevan, whose book *In Place of Fear* crystallized such thought as the party could muster. But the very title reveals the weakness of the book. He was at war with the evils of the past and had little constructive to say about the future. Nothing is more revealing than his advice (pp. 6–7) to other working-class members of Parliament. They must not be daunted by the architecture and decor of the Palace of Westminster. It is the duty of each to resist the atmosphere and cherish 'the deep antagonisms which exist in society'.

The first thing he should bear in mind is that these [the portraits and statues] were not his ancestors. His forebears had no part in the past, the accumulated dust of which now muffles his own footfalls. His forefathers were tending sheep or ploughing the land, or serving the statesmen whose names he sees written on the walls around him, or whose portraits look down upon him in the long corridors. It is not the past of his people that extends in colourful pageantry before his eyes. They were shut out from all this; were forbidden to take part in the dramatic scenes depicted in these frescoes. In him his people are there for the first time, and the history he will make will not be merely an episode in the story he is now reading. It must be wholly different; so different as is the social status which he now brings with him . . .[9]

The errors in this exhortation are too numerous to list but the first and most obvious derives from his failure to look at the building itself. Whatever else he was, he can never have been a craftsman. His forebears had no part in the past? Who then carved the stones and shaped the timbers? Who made the glass and wove the cloth? Who painted the frescoes and who cast Big Ben? The forefathers of the Labour politicians; and the forefathers, incidentally, of half the Tory politicians. Charles Barry, the architect, was no aristocrat, to begin with, nor were many of the statesmen who are there portrayed. What was Cardinal Wolsey by birth and what was Thomas

9. Aneurin Bevan, *In Place of Fear*. London, 1952.

Becket? What was Cobden or Bright, Disraeli or Asquith? But apart from that, the Labour M.P. cannot help but inherit what the older statesmen left behind. There is Parliament itself and the whole structure of administration. That it is mostly obsolete may be the fact, but Bevan had no scheme for its reform. He was a perceptive critic in many ways. He could appreciate the character of Edwardian society. He could write very justly of the 'daily parade of functionless wealth'. He could deplore, and properly, the price of paper and the concentration of newspaper ownership. He could point out, as he did, that fifty journals had ceased publication in 1915. 'Of all monopolies', he wrote, 'monopoly of opinion is the worst. . . . The British people have never been less informed about what is happening in the rest of the world . . . [and] . . . the career of journalism no longer offers adequate opportunities for high quality work.'[10] All this is perfectly true, but what is his remedy? Not socialism but a cheap substitute for paper! Here is a political problem which admits of a political solution but Bevan's approach was that of the capitalist he planned to destroy. Should the press be nationalized, as in Soviet Russia? Admitting that 'a mixed economy is what most people of the West would prefer' and that 'The Victory of socialism need not be universal to be decisive',[11] Bevan left his readers to find a solution for themselves. The problem remains and is with us still.

Where Bevan was most illuminating was in his comment on the collapse of Liberalism after its feeble effort 'to harvest social discontents' for electoral purposes. He pointed out that the House of Commons elected in 1929 was the first elected on the basis of complete adult suffrage. 'Once that had been accomplished, Liberalism was emptied of its historical purpose.'[12] Failing the appearance of another Jeremy Bentham, that was the approximate truth. What Bevan failed to observe is that the Labour Party was also emptied, by 1950, of its historical purpose. In so far as the early socialists had

10. op. cit., pp. 95 and 165.
11. ibid., p. 116.
12. ibid., p. 94.

agreed on a programme, it had been carried out. 'The will to Socialism', wrote G. D. H. Cole in 1935, 'is based on a lively sense of wrongs crying for redress.' Full employment and social security had destroyed, by 1950, the urge to rebel against squalor and injustice. All the old arguments had become inapplicable, all the old statistics had been superseded and all the old plans had been either realized or discarded. Failing another Sidney Webb, the Labour Party had lost its sense of purpose. Roy Jenkins could publish his *Pursuit of Progress* in 1953, but could hardly claim to have overtaken it. 'The days of the giants seem over', wrote Bernard Crick. 'Even a handful of young angries and a quorum of old Marxists boiled together in an anthology do not emerge as one giant . . .'[13] Intellectually, the Labour Party is dead.

13. Bernard Crick, 'Socialist Literature in the 1950's'. Quoted in *The Political Quarterly*, Vol. XXIV, 1953, p. 361.

9

LOOKING BACK IN ANGER

THE Labour Party's defeat in 1951 caused only a minor shock at the time, for the leaders were happier in opposition and the backbenchers could only blame the electorate for its lack of perception. As time went on, however, the lack of inspiration became painfully obvious. Mr Hugh Gaitskell did what he could at this point, naming insecurity, inefficiency and injustice as the economic evils he was to overcome. Only in the classless society would they disappear, and then only as the result of 'a very substantial degree of public intervention, control and ownership'. At the same time he emphasized that nationalization was to be regarded as a means rather than an aim.[1] Mr John Strachey went rather further than that but failed to arouse much excitement over this issue. What was needed, in fact, was a new textbook of socialist theory. None appeared, however, until after the General Election of 1955 in which the Labour vote dropped by 2 per cent. Such disunity had been caused within the party by the advocates of unilateral disarmament that the appearance of a work entitled *The Future of British Socialism* (London, 1956) seemed, if anything, overdue. Its author, moreover, Mr C. A. R. Crosland (Highgate and Trinity, Oxford), had written a better book than any published on this theme since the end of World War II. If there exists an authoritative study of British socialism, this would appear to be it.

Crosland assumes, to begin with, that the national shift to the left is permanent; that the Conservatives, in other words, are more or less socialist. The intervention of the State in economic affairs has thus come to be accepted, and whereas Laski wrote in 1937 that 'political power will, in

1. *The Political Quarterly*, 1953, p. 6.

fact, belong to the owners of economic power',[2] all our experience goes to prove the exact opposite. The capitalists' sinister influence has gone (in so far as it ever existed) and the Conservatives are not even attempting to revive it. So what, Crosland asks, is socialism about?

... The Labour Party has not yet given a clear answer to this question: indeed no one who has observed the Party since 1951, furiously searching for its lost soul, can have failed to sense a mood of deep bewilderment. This mood is in no way discreditable. In the light of the legislative accomplishment, there is no help to be got from searching the files of Transport House; while in view of the change in the balance of economic power, most pre-war analyses have lost their relevance, and the much-thumbed guidebooks of the past must now be thrown away. It is small wonder, in these circumstances, that the approach to a new policy should be fumbling and hesitant, and that there should be a note of irritation both about the demands for 'new thinking,' and then about the responses to it once it comes.[3]

The first instinct, we are told, is to go back to first principles – as Aneurin Bevan had tried to do and without success. Mr Crosland makes the attempt[4] and lists the following points of classical doctrine:

1) Rent, interest and profit should belong to the community.
2) Antagonism and competition should be replaced by Co-operation.
3) Labour is entitled to the whole value of what it produces.
4) The pursuit of private gain is wicked.
5) The means of production should belong to the State.
6) Increased land values should go to the State.
7) People should not labour merely for profit.
8) Poverty, distress, want and squalor should be alleviated not by individual charity but by the State.
9) Trade unions should share in the control of industry.

2. *Liberty in the Modern State*. London, 1930.
3. *The Future of British Socialism*, p. 79.
4. ibid., p. 81.

10) Progress depends upon planning and private enterprise is basically inefficient.

11) All men are equal in status and should be members
of a democratic and classless society.

12) The individual is entitled to freedom.

The author agrees that some of these points have lost their
relevance, and others seem less urgent. Co-operation without
incentive has not been a complete success; (12) is not particularly socialist and people feel less strongly now about (3),
(4), (5) and (9). Experience with nationalized industries does
not go to prove that they are free from dispute; (7) was only
a vague aspiration from the start; and the Trade Unions have
done little to press their claim under (9). The points which
seem to retain their validity are (6), (8), (10), (11) and –possibly – (5). Many non-socialists would agree, however, on
(6) and (10), and relatively few socialists now insist on (5).

The two remaining aspirations – the concern with social welfare,
and the desire for an equal and classless society – still have a perfectly clear relevance. The first implies an acceptance of collective responsibility and an extremely high priority for the relief
of social distress or misfortune. . . .The relief of this distress
and the elimination of this squalor is the main object of social
expenditure; and a socialist is identified as one who wishes to give
this an exceptional priority over the claims on resources. This is
not a matter of the overall vertical equality of incomes; the arguments are humanitarian and compassionate, not egalitarian. It
is a matter of priorities in the distribution of the national output, and a belief that the first priority should always be given to
the poor, the unfortunate, the 'have-nots', and generally to those
in need; from which follows a certain view about collective
social responsibility, and thence about the role of the state
and the level of taxation. This represents the first major difference
between a socialist and a conservative.

The second distinctive socialist ideal is social equality and the
'class society'. The socialist seeks a distribution of rewards, status
and privileges egalitarian enough to minimize social resentment,
to secure justice between individuals, and to equalize opportunities; and he seeks to weaken the existing deep-seated class

stratification, with its concomitant feelings of envy and inferiority, and its barriers of uninhibited mingling between the classes. This belief in social equality which has been the strongest ethical inspiration of virtually every socialist doctrine still remains the most characteristic feature of socialist thought today.[5]

Mr Crosland sees, as many socialists do not, that a theoretical argument for equality has never been provided. The case no longer rests (he agrees) on the need to take from the rich before we can relieve the poor. On what then does it rest? He argues that inequalities lead to envy and resentment, that appointments and promotions are made for the wrong reasons and that social divisions are wasteful and inefficient. Leaders are chosen badly and there is a waste of talent because 'clever working-class children are still denied access to the public schools'. He considers, nevertheless, that there are limits to the degree of equality, which is desirable. 'We do not want complete equality of incomes, since extra responsibility and exceptional talent require and deserve a differential reward.'[6] The Rt Hon. Mr C. A. R. Crosland, M.P., (in 1967, £8,500 a year) is emphatic on the need for differentials. In many other respects his views are moderate. He wants neither to close the grammar schools nor to nationalize the aircraft industry. He argues, finally, that efficiency has little to do with ownership in the modern company because ownership has little to do with control.

As an analysis of the known facts, *The Future of British Socialism* is admirable. As a new revelation it fails for a number of reasons. So far from containing a new idea, it merely admits that most of the old ideas are obsolete. And of the two ideas which remain, neither can be thought impressive. To give the first priority to poor relief may be humanitarian – although quite obviously wrong – but this is in any case a question of degree. As for the argument about inequalities leading to resentment and envy, the fallacy is manifest. It is the socialist who tells the working man to feel resentful. When the workman heeds this prompting, his envy becomes the fact upon which the argument is to rest.

5. *The Future of British Socialism*, p. 112.   6. ibid., p. 190.

This is the sort of reasoning which could justify anything, from rape to nuclear bombing. As a guide for future policy this book amounts, therefore, to nothing. Our new Moses descends from the mountain with something far short of the ten (or twelve) commandments. Emerging from the cloud he has merely to confess that ten of the original dozen have been repealed, that the one of the two which remain is a matter of priorities and that the last should not be taken too literally. There is in this, we must admit, an element of anticlimax. The Chosen People are left somewhat at a loss.

There are other (if minor) prophets, however, whose revelations may be more exciting. In 1958, for example, there appeared a book called *Conviction* edited by Norman Mackenzie, and offering scope to the younger men.[7] In it Mr Peter Shore admits that public and private enterprise have become indistinguishable, while Mr Raymond Williams proclaims that 'Culture is ordinary'. Mr Peter Townsend finds to his dismay that 'People believe that there are no just causes left'; and this despite the fact that the unemployed are relatively worse off in 1958 than they were in 1938 – or, for that matter, in 1912. Mr Nigel Calder considers that our obsession has been with 'backward-looking reform not forward-looking change' but raises more questions than he cares to answer. Mr Mervyn Jones remarks that the Labour Party has never had a foreign policy but that a revival of 'Socialist pacificism' would be a possible substitute. Mr Paul Johnson believes that a socialist society must involve a break in historical continuity. He would therefore abolish the Monarchy, the House of Lords, the Public Schools, the Colleges at Oxford and Cambridge, the Church of England, the Inns of Court and the Honours List. His most interesting proposal is the one since adopted; to destroy 'Service' tradition by amalgamating the forces. He concludes, finally, that the Labour Party must recover its sense of outrage, something quite distinct from a love of power. Iris Murdoch complains that British socialist theory died with Laski and Tawney and

7. *Conviction*. ed. Norman Mackenzie. London, 1958. See pp. 17, 18, 49, 87, 96, 100–3, 144–7, 165, 183, 198, 216, 229, 230–2.

that all subsequent literature is merely technical, lacking any analysis even of the equality concept 'which is, in fact, in danger of becoming the only influential "general idea" of contemporary Socialism'. The proletariat, in her opinion, still exists, 'a deracinate, disinherited and excluded mass of people' who no longer think of themselves as deprived. Her remedy is to revive Guild Socialism, give work its old significance and seek inspiration in 'ideas which were common to Marx and to William Morris'. No single contribution has anything constructive to suggest or any idea which is not obviously derivative, and the break in historical continuity which Mr Paul Johnson recommends is inapplicable, apparently, to the Labour Party itself. All else is to go but the London School of Economics is to remain. Like the other contributors, Mr Paul Johnson has nothing to offer of later date than 1894. So far as the future is concerned, his mind is blank.

Can the same be said of the Rt Hon. R. H. S. Crossman, M.P. (Winchester and New College)? His book[8] is more, certainly, than an admission of mental blackout. He analyses, for example, the process by which the public has achieved a 'fatuous complacency' about western capitalism in its British form. Discussing the issue of nationalization – often considered as obsolete – he points out that the communist countries still regard this 'as the first step towards planning a balanced economic development'. The Affluent Society may seem more attractive but the fact remains that,

. . . in terms of military power, of industrial development, of technological advance, of mass literacy and, eventually of mass consumption too, the planned Socialist economy, as exemplified in the Communist States, is proving its capacity to outpace and overtake the wealthy and comfortable Western economies. (pp. 8-9)

He predicts that Russian productivity will exceed that of the United States by the late 70s and that of Britain long before. He maintains that western affluence had been achieved by 'scamping vital public services and imposing gross injustices' on the sick and the old. And while all the affluent societies 'keep capital investment down to a dangerously

8. *Labour in the Affluent Society*. Fabian Tract 325, 1960, p. 8.

low level', Britain is the weakest in this respect. Our improvement in productivity thus lags behind that of Germany, France and even Italy. 'Squeezed between three giants – the United States, the Common Market and the Communist bloc', Britain's standard of living may actually fall. Our Affluent Society fails to provide sufficiently for education, welfare, science, defence or health.

That is why we can predict with mathematical certainty that, as long as the public sector of industry remains the minority sector throughout the Western world, we are bound to be defeated in every kind of peaceful competition which we undertake with the Russians and the Eastern bloc. . .

The idea that we can achieve the same ends by leaving the great concerns in private hands and controlling their development from Whitehall is as illusory as the concept that their profits can be taxed to pay for the Welfare State. We are faced with a sharp choice. Either we accept the Affluent Society as we know it, including the limitations on State activity and public spending that it implies . . . [letting the Labour Party wither away, or else we must] present an outright Socialist challenge to the Affluent Society and give warning of the coming crisis.[9]

Reluctant to see the Labour Party disintegrate, the author proposes to ensure 'that the public dominates over the private sector'. This means the transfer of power to the State. At this point Mr Crossman observes, rather belatedly, the decline of Parliament, the decay of the Cabinet and the rise of a top level bureaucracy (also largely from Winchester and New College) which is itself a threat to freedom. He concludes, rather lamely, that something should be done about it. What he fails to see is that the political reform is the *first* step; without which the economic and social problems cannot even be properly discussed.

What other ideas have the Socialists to put forward? Typical of their output is Fabian Tract 326,[10] in which the authors define what they regard as the key problems of the day. These

9. *Labour in the Affluent Society*. Fabian Tract 325, 1960, p. 22.
10. Wayland and Elizabeth Young, *The Socialist Imagination*. London, 1960.

are (1) Money, (2) Advertising, (3) Transport, (4) Caste, (5) Colonial Policy and (6) The Bomb. In considering (1) they suggest that finance experts have become too important as compared with engineers, teachers and artists. They regard with horror (2), a whole industry devoted to increasing consumption among the satisfied while people overseas are starving. They deal with (3) by Planning and (4) by Comprehensive Schools. Colour prejudice is the heart of problem (5), dealt with by following the example of Brazil and Hawaii, and as regards (6) they are – with a touch of originality – against it. To judge from this sort of literature the Socialist Imagination does not amount to much. The only significant development is in relation to the Black Commonwealth. The old theme of rescuing the poor – Underdoggery for short – is now applied to students from overseas and coloured immigrants and so, by a natural extension to the countries (quick, the atlas!) from which these presumably distressed people have come. This is not a topic on which the Trade Unions can be relied upon to feel the same way as the intellectuals. It represents, nevertheless, a departure from Labour Party tradition. A party which was opposed to the British Empire in its heyday is now enthusiastic about the Afro-Asian ghost which gibbers on its tomb. It remains a question, however, whether these emotions are based upon knowledge or ignorance.

We are brought back to Mr Crosland as the pale successor to Beatrice and Sidney Webb. But who has succeeded George Bernard Shaw? Doyen of left-wing authors is Mr J. B. Priestley (born 1894), whose best work was done between 1929 and 1950. His influence has dwindled since then and he has for long been a figure of the past. How fares by contrast the *modern* literature of the Left? There is much talk of socialist culture, going back to Mr H. S. Morrison's Festival of Britain in 1951. The real spate of left-wing authorship followed, however, the Labour Party's electoral defeat in 1955 and the attempted Revolution in Hungary of 1956. Exclusion from office combined with disillusion about Russia to produce a mood of cynicism. This was exemplified in the literature

and drama of the 'Kitchen Sink' and notably in John Osborne's play, *Look Back in Anger*, first performed at the
Royal Court Theatre in 1956. Marxism is implicit in much
of the dialogue, and Jimmy Porter, the central character,
states that his father fought in Spain. Another character says
of Jimmy, 'He doesn't know where he is, or where he's
going. He'll never do anything, and he'll never amount to
anything.' This remains approximately true of the author,
whose subsequent plays include *A Subject of Scandal and
Concern* (performed on the radio, 1960), the hero of which
is a socialist prosecuted for blasphemy in 1842, and *The
Blood of the Bambergs,* first performed at the Royal Court
Theatre in 1962. This latter play, staged at this significantly
named playhouse, is an attack on the monarchy; as also on
the late Mr Richard Dimbleby as the B.B.C.'s commentator
on state occasions. Harold Pinter's play *The Birthday Party*
was first presented at the Arts Theatre, Cambridge, in 1958
and followed an earlier play as gloomy, called *The Caretaker*.
Mr J. B. Priestley says of this dramatist that 'generally with
Mr Pinter, menace is on its way, messages are mysteriously
seeping through but they always contain bad news'.[11] In
Arnold Wesker's play *Roots,* second play of the Chicken
Soup trilogy, first performed at Coventry in 1959, the characters are Norfolk peasants of whom Mr Bernard Levin writes, 'The villain in *Roots* is the society that treads these
people into the dirt.' A character in this play confesses that
'We don't fight for anything, we're so mentally lazy we
might as well be dead.... The whole stinkin' commercial
world insults us and we don't care a damn.... We want the
Third rate – we got it!' This fact is further illustrated in
Chips with Everything, first performed at the Royal Court
Theatre in 1962; a play about the R.A.F. This trend in
literature continues and is paralleled by the same sense of
frustration shown in painting, sculpture and music. Miss
Jennie Lee exemplifies the Labour Party's interest in culture,
but it is not the left-wing products that people generally like.
The art which expresses mere frustration is of historical

11. *New Statesman,* 23 April 1965.

interest but has little appeal to average folk and none, of course, to the young.

The technical skill of these authors, or of some of them, is considerable, but they are well below George Bernard Shaw in stature. Apart from that, however, they differ from him in knowledge and outlook. Shaw, whatever his faults may have been, had always done his homework. Behind his most challenging paradoxes there lurked a concealed battery of blue-books and statistical data. These later socialists are relatively ill-informed, knowing enough to voice a grievance but never enough to suggest a remedy. Quite apart from that, moreover, their sense of disappointment extends to the Labour Party itself. Current satire directed against the 'Establishment' involves the discovery that the Trade Unions have become a part of it. A few satirists have even noticed the Hereditary Leaders of Democracy; the second generation Lloyd Georges and MacDonalds, the family background of the Jenkins, and the Browns. The left-wing Establishment has come to be symbolized by Lord Snow, the socialist leader with a son at Eton. Other Labour politicians have been more cautious but Mr Douglas Jay (Winchester and New College) sent two sons to his old school, where Sir Frank Soskice (St Paul's and Balliol) also sent his son. Even more than the Conservatives the Labour Party look to Oxford (not to Cambridge) for their talent. Twenty of their Ministers are from Oxford, five from Balliol and three each from Magdalen and New College. The picture emerges of a socialist hierarchy with its own family and academic traditions, its own type of stuffy conservatism. Arnold Wesker makes this point in his play *I'm talking about Jerusalem,* first performed at Coventry in 1960:

Ronnie . . . We put a Labour Party in Power. . . . But what did the bleeders do, eh? They sang the Red Flag in Parliament and then started building atom bombs. Lunatics! Raving lunatics! And a whole generation of us laid down our arms and retreated into ourselves, a whole generation.

Retreat they may have done, leaving Liverpool to the Beatles, but the left-wing intelligentsia has its own hierarchy of which Centre 43 (at Chalk Farm) is supposed to be the Ark of the Covenant. Its sponsors range from Graham Greene to Vanessa Redgrave, from Peter Sellers to Lord Snow, and it is founded on the principle that 'All art finally must be available free to the community.' We are not told why. What *is* made abundantly clear is that this ultimate aim can be achieved only by current subscription. To this extent Arnold Wesker is at least doing something practical. John Osborne typifies, rather, those who have retreated into themselves. His views are well summarized in his letter to *Tribune* of 18 August, 1961. '*To my fellow countrymen,*' it begins, 'This is a letter of hate.' The truth of this claim becomes apparent as the letter continues:

My hatred for you is almost the only constant satisfaction you have left me. My favourite fantasy is four minutes or so non-commercial viewing as you fry in your democratically elected hot seat in Westminster, preferably with your condoning democratic constituents.

There is murder in my brain, and I carry a knife in my heart for every one of you. Macmillan, and you, Gaitskell, you particularly...

The significance of this outburst is that the Labour Party had become (for Osborne and for the generation to which Wesker refers) a part of the Establishment. Converse of the process by which the Conservatives moved half-way towards socialism, the socialists have now developed a conservatism of their own. They have moved symbolically from the London School of Economics to Balliol. It was in this new guise that the Labour Party returned to power in 1964, bringing with them the querulous attitudes of the Oxford Union.

10

THE PARTY LINE

MR HAROLD WILSON (born 1916), who became the Labour Party's leader after Mr Hugh Gaitskell's death in 1963, has the right background for a left-wing politician. His origin is in puritanical West Yorkshire and Lancashire. Baptist or Congregational, his subsequent moves have been from Merseyside to Oxford (Jesus College: Philosophy, Politics and Economics) and from there to Whitehall. He was in early and close contact with Sir William Beveridge and Mr G. D. H. Cole, his original taste for Sunday School and the Boy Scouts giving place to studies of unemployment and the Colne Valley Co-operative Movement. His wartime experience was in the Ministries of Supply, Labour, Fuel and Power, his notable achievement being the plan he perfected for nationalizing the Coal Industry. Elected M.P. for Ormskirk in 1945, his first ministerial post was at the Ministry of Works, his first cabinet office that of President, after Cripps, of the Board of Trade. He thus knits together the characteristics of the puritan, the Fabian economist, the bureaucrat and the planner. His typical plea is for 'a sense of economic purpose' and 'a social purpose', but to this he added in 1964, a concern for 'the standing of Britain in the world', based upon the black as opposed to the white Commonwealth. He believes in Progress, and in 1945 quoted with approval the lines 'England arise, the long, long night is over.' It is not improbable that he really believes this, taking his cue from Mr Aneurin Bevan (see p. 125) with whom he was closely associated in 1951. More than anyone else he voices the Labour Party's outlook and policy, and his book *The Relevance of British Socialism* (London, 1964) contains the gists of what he has to say.

In this work he describes the acrimonious dispute which

followed the Party's renewed defeat in 1959. Lacking any new idea of substance, the party leaders were then in the mood, some of them, to jettison the sole idea in which they had all believed. This was contained in Clause IV of the Party's Constitution, which defines its most typical aim in these words:

To secure for the workers by hand or by brain the full fruits of their industry and the most equitable distribution thereof that may be possible, upon the basis of the common ownership of the means of production, distribution and exchange, and the best obtainable system of popular administration and control of each industry or service.... Generally to promote the political, social and economic emancipation of the people, and more particularly of those who depend directly upon the exertions by hand or by brain for the means of life...

In view of the indifferent performance of the nationalized industries, this article of faith had rather lost its appeal. The National Executive dared not delete it, however, preferring to add a further explanation. This was accepted at the annual Conference and remains the official doctrine. 'The British Labour Party', it begins, 'is a democratic socialist party. Its central idea is the brotherhood of man ...' Clauses 1 to 4 cover the topics of Equality, Anti-Imperialism, the United Nations and help for the Under-Developed Countries of the World. Clause 9 calls for Democracy in Industry, Clause 11 resists arbitrary power and the glorification of the State, and Clause 12 reiterates the Party's belief in democratic institutions. The more important clauses, 5, 6, 7 and 8, read as follows:

5. It [the Party] stands for social justice, for a society in which the claims of those in hardship or distress come first; where the wealth produced by all is fairly shared among all; where differences in rewards depend not upon birth or inheritance but on the efforts, skill and creative energy contributed to the common good; and where equal opportunities exist for all to live a full and varied life.

6. Regarding the pursuit of material wealth by and for itself as empty and barren, it rejects the selfish, acquisitive doctrines of

capitalism, and strives to create instead a socialist community based on fellowship, co-operation and service in which all can share fully in our cultural heritage.

7. Its aim is a classless society from which all class barriers and false social values have been eliminated.

8. It holds that to ensure full employment, rising production, stable prices and steadily advancing living standards the nation's economy should be planned and all concentrations of power subordinated to the interests of the community as a whole.

10. It is convinced that these social and economic objectives can be achieved only through an expansion of common ownership substantial enough to give the community power over the commanding heights of the economy. Common ownership takes varying forms including state-owned industries and firms, producer and consumer co-operatives, municipal ownership and public participation in private concerns. Recognizing that both public and private enterprise have a place in the economy it believes that further extension of common ownership should be decided from time to time in the light of these objectives, and according to circumstances, with due regard for the views of the workers and consumers concerned.[1]

In considering these objects it is fair to ask, first of all, how the Labour Party has progressed since 1917 (see p. 87). The phrase about the brotherhood of man goes back to the French Revolution and is based on nothing. Clause 5 repeats the original demand for 'a systematic approach towards a healthy equality of material circumstances', but with a new and more cautious insistence on salary differentials. Clause 6 asks afresh for a social order based not on competition but co-operation. The classless society (Clause 7) of 1964 is merely the 'healthy equality' of 1917. The full employment (Clause 8) of the lastest Manifesto is much like the National Minimum of the first. Clause 10 is a watered-down version of 'The Common Ownership of the Means of Production' and Mr Wilson's economic and social purpose is nothing more than Sidney Webb's 'common purpose' and 'common plan which can be explained and discussed' (but not reversed). In so far as there is novelty it would seem to lie in

1. *The Relevance of British Socialism*, p. 6 et seq.

Mr Wilson's belief that private enterprise has still a part to play in the economy; a belief which we must reconcile as we can with his rejection of 'the selfish, acquisitive doctrines of capitalism'. In other respects the earlier document seems the more modern of the two. Sidney Webb, for one thing, expected the Labour Party to accept the guidance of 'the best Political Science of its time'. There is no mention of this by 1964 but merely a heavy reiteration of the old programme in an English style which has certainly not improved. In about fifty years the Labour Party would seem to have learnt nothing at all; forgetting something, moreover, of what it had originally been told. And these are the words of the concluding summary:

In this book I have set out the Socialist philosophy in terms of economic, technological and social advance. But it is the determination of my colleagues and myself to ensure that the next Labour Government shall go down to history, not only for achievement in these fields, but as one of the great liberal reforming administrations of this or any other century. . .[2]

In discussing this 'Socialist philosophy', we do well to begin with Clause 5 in which social justice is given a high priority. A society is to be created in which 'the claims of those in hardship or distress come first'. Implicit in this 'philosophy' is the rejection of any aim external to the society which is being planned. Societies of the past have bent their efforts to save their civilization from barbarism, to create beauty in every form, to uphold the true religion, to spread the blessings of law and order, to rescue the Holy Sepulchre, to seek a New World overseas, to abolish slavery or win eternal fame. The Labour Party, by contrast, is concerned only with itself. We have here an army which is dedicated to the care of its own wounded. And the odd thing is that even the wounded would recover sooner if the campaign had some object. From the same clause we learn that income differentials will be based on merit and that all shall have equal opportunities to achieve, not political power, but 'a full and varied life', with a share (Clause 6) in 'our cul-

2. op. cit., p. 108.

tural heritage'. Central to this programme is the demand (Clause 7) for a classless society; something more than has been achieved in Russia. But what are the 'false social values'? We see from Clause 5 that some people may expect a higher salary as reward for creative energy and skill (if used for the common good), but these must not develop the sort of values that would separate them from their less gifted neighbours. How are they to be prevented? And what is to happen, meanwhile, to Earl Attlee and the House of Lords? Does the Peerage represent false social values? Do the Orders of Knighthood? Does the Order, more particularly, of the British Empire, of which Mr Harold Wilson is an Officer? If military rank represents a false social value (as it presumably must) how is it to be destroyed? And what of the respect that may be accorded to an Honorary Fellow of both University and New College, Oxford? We are not told what values are false nor in what their falsity consists. Still less are we told of the means by which they are to be eliminated.

Clause 8 deals with planning the economy and ensuring that 'all concentrations of power' should be subordinate to the interests of the (British) community. What is implicit here is that the national must always predominate over the international interest. It is obvious that the concentrations of power to which this clause relates are mostly international; the oil companies being a case in point. Consistently pursued, the object of this clause would be to destroy what international institutions there are. For a model of co-operation between the different peoples of the world we should look, first of all, to the banks, to the Bourse, and the boardroom of Shell. To found a genuinely international airline would do more for the world as a whole than could anything done by the United Nations. To improve the relationships between peoples the first step is to multiply the institutions which are *not* national. The objects of the Labour Party are to drag everything down to the merely national level. 'We are not a flag-waving party,' said Mr Wilson at Scarborough, 'but we are a deeply patriotic party . . .'[3] This is true: and often, one

3. op. cit., p. 82.

might add, appallingly true. If we are ever to progress beyond the present concepts of nationality, we must realize first of all that to nationalize what is even potentially international is a step in the wrong direction.

With Clause 10 we come back to the Labour Party's obsession with 'common ownership', a concept based upon confusion between ownership and control. In the modern world, as Mr Crosland himself has pointed out, control rests with the management and will do so in any case, whether the enterprise is 'public' or 'private'. After an industrial organization has been nationalized or partly nationalized, it may be regarded as a public service (in which case it will normally be run at a loss) or it may remain in competitive business. If a further extension of public ownership means that more and more businesses are to be run at a loss, like the railways, the whole economy must finally collapse. We must assume, therefore, that a majority of state-owned plants must be run at a profit to the nation. That decision made, the public ownership remains, but the responsibility to Parliament has gone. It is quite possible for the Minister to say, 'This is how the business is to be run, with wages and prices as laid down by me – and never mind what loss may result.' But the Minister who says 'Make a fair profit on the investment' has lost control at that instant. For the directors who are to make a profit must obviously do it their own way. If they are responsible for the investment, they are not responsible to the Minister nor he to Parliament. To say, 'Do it my way *and* show a profit' would be lunacy and the more so in that the Minister does not even remain long enough in office. So the whole idea of public ownership is irrelevant to the problems of the day. For the community to assume power over the commanding heights of the economy a transfer of ownership is at once needless and ineffective, for the power can be had without ownership and the ownership without power. As for public participation in private enterprise, we may doubt whether any government would play fair. Governments which tax oil so as to make state-owned coal more marketable are not going to see any public enterprise go bankrupt in open competition with a privately-owned rival. The dice will be loaded before the game begins and no sane person would expect it to be otherwise.

So what does the Labour Party's programme amount to? When confronted by the great issues of the day, the Party is virtually speechless. Its spokesmen have nothing to say about over-population, about the renascent Orient or about the Bomb. They have little interest in Britain's entry into a United Europe. They have no political theory and no plan for modernizing our political system. They lay no emphasis on saving our cities or our countryside. Faced by an appalling lack of infantry, their first idea is to disband the Territorial Army. Accepting a need to defend the Commonwealth in South-east Asia, they hasten to dispense with the aircraft carriers upon which such a defence must presumably rely. Mr Wilson's expressed concern for the standing of Britain in the world turns out to be little more than a hope that his social programme will be an inspiration to other nations. This seems scarcely plausible, for nations with higher productivity can afford to spend more on welfare; as indeed on everything. Through all the Labour Party's thinking runs an obsession with economics and a distrust of policies based upon anything else. In this the Conservatives are too apt to follow the socialist lead. Their objections to socialism are seldom sufficiently basic. It is interesting, nevertheless, to find what their reactions are. Interviewed fairly recently, Mr Enoch Powell deplored the absurdity of economic planning and *exhortations* to do things 'in the public interest' — as influenced but not as legally compelled. The idealized and benevolent 'State' is, to Mr Powell, a myth, its eternal weakness lying in the fact that its decisions are unpredictable. Apart from that, the Labour Party refuses to see and admit the breakdown of socialism in Russia. Interviewed in the same way, Mr Quintin Hogg thought that the Labour Party is at its worst and most doctrinaire in local government. On the national level its faults range from a moral indignation, which singles out South Africa and Spain while silent over Cuba and Tibet, to a drab philistinism which is far worse than the older puritanism from which it derives. To Mr Eldon Griffiths the Socialists are killjoys who sing the 'Red Flag' and 'Jerusalem', who talk like secular curates but are otherwise the dreariest of organization men. Mr David Howell considers that the Labour Party is running out of intellectual capital. From nonconformity it has inherited a belief in the power of exhortation, even to the point of raising productivity by propaganda. These are valid points against the Labour Party but the Conservatives' failure is in having no policy of their own; or none at least which is unrelated to socialism. Upon them, too, Marxism has had its influence.

Come, finally, to the General Election of 1966. The Labour Party's manifesto bore the title *Time for Decision,* and here, if anywhere, we should look for evidence of thought. It is, however, the unfortunate tendency of the age for political parties to seek professional advice in drafting their election propaganda. As competent public relations consultants will all give the same advice, each party manifesto comes to look much like any other. The Socialists and Conservatives of 1966 were thus unanimous in promising the voter a sound economy with help for industry and agriculture, a rising standard of living, more housing and better transport, replanned cities and a preserved countryside, better welfare, health and education facilities, fairer taxation, more policemen, war on (overseas) want and support for China's admission to the United Nations. The chief originality on the Conservative side lay in a promise to reduce taxes, establish an Industrial Court, set up a Recreation Department and preserve the Territorial Army. More daring still, the Conservatives also borrowed from the Liberals the idea of autonomy, or at least a greater measure of independence, for Scotland and Wales. In what did the Labour Party reveal its imagination? It promised to support the United Nations, in which the Conservatives had lost interest. It promised to reduce defence costs and internationalize its nuclear weapons. It promised to discover 'the best ways of integrating the Public Schools into the State sector' of education. It promised, finally, to modernize Parliament; partly by broadcasting debates, partly by giving the vote to people aged eighteen, and partly again by curtailing still further the powers of the House of Lords. It is on the political side of the programme that the wording is most vague, the reinforcement of 'the demo-cratic element in modern Government' being more precise, if anything, than the improvements, as foreshadowed, in 'procedure and the work of committees'.[4]

It is not to our present purpose to ask whether the Labour Party had more or less to offer than their opponents. What we need to discuss is their progress in thought since the death of Sidney Webb. They were offering to legislate, remember, for a Britain which had suffered drastic change in a dramatic-ally changing world. Crippled by casualties and the cost of war, with its influence reduced and its Empire gone, Britain was facing an uncertain future in the midst of a scientific revolution and a new balance of power. What was the Lab-our Party's response? It's first idea was to weaken the House of Lords, catching up again with the mood of 1911. Its sec-ond idea was to widen the franchise; taking us back to 1929, if not to 1832. More hopeful than these quaint anachronisms was the talk of modernizing Parliament; which meant no more, however, than some adjustments in committee work and procedure. To reduce defence costs and weaken the Royal Navy was an automatic reaction to danger, exactly repeating the political scene of the 1930s, not to mention that which followed the conclusion of the Seven Years War in 1763. To disband the Territorial Army was the natural sequel to its having saved Britain in the two previous wars. This pro-posal came readily from the party once dominated by Lans-bury and the pacifists and showed no particular awareness of the current scene whether in South Vietnam or Los An-geles. There was nothing in the economic and welfare pro-posals which Sidney Webb could not have dictated in his sleep. Enthusiasm for the United Nations was a dream going back to 1920, and the case for subsidizing the arts was put more eloquently by George Bernard Shaw. There was noth-ing in the Labour Party programme, in fact, which reflected

4. *Time for Decision.* Manifesto of the Labour Party, 1966.

anything which had happened for the previous thirty years. The country was offered afresh the unchanged ideas of 1894 and the changeless programme of 1917. What was most significant in the manifesto was perhaps the sequence of its paragraphs. The plea was, in this order, for a strong economy, for housing, for welfare, for a wider democracy and for world peace. As a matter of priorities there would have been something to say for taking this agenda in the reverse order. Against this, however, was a tradition going back to 1847. On this subject Karl Marx must have his way even now.

If there was anything revolutionary in the Labour Party's manifesto it lay, perhaps, in the proposal to broadcast 'Commons proceedings in order to bring Parliament closer to the people it represents, and to increase the sense of public participation in policy making'. The unconscious humour of this proposal lies, first of all, in the loose identification of the House of Commons with Parliament. Why should the Lords be less televised? Because their standard of debate is obviously higher? Because they are more representative, as they plainly are? Or because Lord Attlee has said for a lifetime what Mr Wilson is saying now? In the event, the Commons have refused to be televised while the Lords have consented. Whatever may be decided hereafter on this point, the broadcasting of Commons debates might, in one sense, be worth while. It would be salutary for Members of Parliament to know how they rated, as entertainment, on the popularity scale. As apart from that, the immediate loss of efficiency would be a small matter as compared with the advantage of even a few folk deciding, occasionally, to listen or view. What would the result be of people realizing the truth – that the House of Commons is a tedious and time-wasting machine which has lost its authority and purpose? Would they enjoy 'the sense of public participation in policy making'? Or would they perceive that the policy (where there is any) has been decided elsewhere and that their participation is a dreary irrelevance, the stifling boredom of which defies description? In this one proposal, if in no other, might lie the seeds of revolution. The situation is well defined in Scene II of *Saint Joan*:

THE ARCHBISHOP: . . . Could you make our citizens pay war taxes, or our soldiers sacrifice their lives, if they knew what was really happening instead of what seems to them to be happening?

LA TREMOUILLE: No, by Saint Dennis: the fat would be in the fire before sundown.

THE ARCHBISHOP: Would it not be quite easy to tell them the truth?

LA TREMOUILLE: Man alive, they wouldn't believe it.[5]

That they would not believe it is still the fact. With the proceedings televised, incredulity might turn to amazement and wrath and what happened before sundown might be interesting to see.

5. G. Bernard Shaw, *Saint Joan*, Scene II.

THE CLASSLESS SOCIETY

WHILE the Labour Party can derive little inspiration from its Trade Unions and Co-operative Societies, its intellectuals still point the way to a glorious future. Central to their idea of progress is the classless society. In the world as they want to see it, incomes will not be equal but everyone will have an equal chance to gain managerial position. 'We are building the New Britain', claimed Mr Harold Wilson in 1965, and the classless society was part, at least, of what he had to offer. In contemplating this ideal, initial doubt must centre upon the problem of energy, whether individual or national. If we are to rule out the more obvious types of incentive, we are left with people who have no reason to do more than they must. In the great period of British expansion the national purpose was served by the more or less selfish efforts of the individual. All our experience suggests that the individual thwarted in his fortune-seeking will either do nothing or will develop an undesirable taste for power. Almost the only exceptions to the rule are celibate priests and monks, trained in the service of a powerful missionary religion. But even Trappists, Jesuits or Communists will succumb, at times, to the lure of idleness or intrigue. Ordinary men need an ordinary incentive and the greater the reward, and the heavier the penalty for failure, the more they will do to achieve success. It is the sum total of these private efforts which creates, when properly harnessed, the drive towards any national purpose that may be generally agreed. The country is most dynamic when the forces of class or individual ambition have scope to develop their maximum power. It is the desperately poor whose urge to escape from poverty will take them, almost at a bound, into the ranks of the affluent. Most ruthless of these, ready to die in the attempt, are those whose family tradition includes some memory of previous rank or fortune. The mere swiftness of the earlier fall will add impetus to the later rise. For them the privileges of position are not merely something they want but something to which they feel entitled.

These individual efforts are confined, however, to a small minority. In any population there is and has always been a vast preponderance of the passive. People who can be so described are not without ambition. They would welcome the fortune which might come to them in a lottery or by a bequest. They are eager to hear of ways in which money can be made or spent. Gambling on football results, they will daydream about the fortune which might possibly result. But for actually making a fortune they lack the energy. In the majority of households the available energy does no more than keep the household going. Each day for most people is like the last, each week is like the week before, each month a repetition of the previous month, each year a tale re-told to an audience which has aged twelve months since the last performance. Men rise, shave and breakfast, travel to work, eat and work again, travel and eat, relax and exercise, make love or quarrel, gamble or read and so to sleep. Women rise, breakfast and cook, wash dishes and make beds, do their shopping and tend their children, cook and eat, gossip, relax and sleep. More fortunate at first, children are soon involved in the same stale sequence with the classrom instead of the factory, with homework instead of play. While the pattern may vary with the income group, the day's routine has captured us all in some degree. We must eat in order to work and work in order to eat. And having done what we must we lack time or energy to do what we want. What effort most people have to spare is negligible. What impetus they had is spent by evening, if not by noon, and what time remains is useless. A minority of people begin with more energy and have something left when the day's work ends. A smaller minority, no more energetic than the average, have a shorter day's routine, leaving time to spare. A tiny minority have both energy and time. For all but this last handful the leisure not absorbed by sleep is mostly given to recreation and sport, hobbies and romance. Out of the same small fraction of life must be taken the time and effort to achieve something more than survival.

Many people, and many readers of this page, will realize that they are themselves passive, easy-going and relaxed. They may argue, moreover, that their happiness derives from this fact and that pushing and striving is bad for the digestion, the temper and the morals. Were everyone the same as they, society would enjoy a quiet stability. Mr Harold Wilson thus offers us, if we will continue to support him, 'a more balanced, satisfied society in which human dignity is accepted as the ultimate aim of economic activity'.[1] Had every community these characteristics the world would be at peace. For those whose belief is in a future life, to which the present is a merely tedious preliminary, this argument may well be conclusive. For the rest of us, however, much that is of value in the world derives from what use we make of our surplus energy after the essential work has been done. True as this may be of the individual or family, it is still more true of the community as a whole. We can fairly ask of any given country: 'What is it doing? What has it done?' Granted the fact of its survival, we reserve our interest and praise for its more positive achievements. These, we find, tend to follow a familiar sequence. In Phase I the political unit (whether city, province or nation) defends itself against external pressure. In Phase II it takes the offensive and establishes its power and influence over a wider area. In Phase III comes the full flowering of a culture already apparent during Phases I and II but now given full scope for development. Military, political and economic success is accompanied and followed by artistic, intellectual, literary and musical achievement. A vast number of individual efforts have gone to make an impressive total. We look back and say, 'That was the country's golden age.'

Are we right to classify societies, groups and families according to their sense of purpose? Are we right to place the passive in what might be thought a lower category? Or

1. *The Relevance of British Socialism*. London, 1964, p. 108.

should we admit that simple and unambitious people can be happy and, quite possibly, wise? Here we run into the difficulty of measuring what we can scarcely even define. We should have learnt, however, from our own experience that there is a difference in quality between the pleasure derived from a holiday and the pleasure derived from having accomplished some considerable task. There is, on the one hand, the sensation of sitting on the beach at Skegness. There is, on the other hand, the sensation of looking down from the summit of the Matterhorn after climbing it in winter by the difficult route. The two states of mind are scarcely comparable. We know, moreover, from our literature that it is the sensation of conquest – or even, for that matter, of failure – which sticks in our memory and finds expression in our verse. Sitting on the seafront at Clacton does not lend itself to the same sort of epic narrative. We can agree, surely, that the satisfaction of having completed a cathedral, an oratorio, a portrait or a tragedy is different in kind. To the pleasure of rest we have added the sense of achievement. As different again is the previous period of work, as anyone must know who has seen troops inactive in camp. Morale rises with the order to march, not because the effort is pleasant but because it renews the sense of purpose. Failing any other yardstick we can fairly assume that the greater works of architecture and music, literature and art express a community's aspirations, triumphs and pride. Judging from all that has survived from past ages, we can readily believe that people are happier when striving to accomplish some tremendous task. Feelings are hard to assess but we have inherited, remember, the chanties they roared at the halyards, the songs they sang on the march. Whatever the background of hardship, these reflect the gaiety of their age. Men might die by the roadside but the army was on the move, 'Over the hills and far away'. The goal might be ill-defined. Few can have doubted, however, that it was there.

With the loss of the Empire the British national purpose was lost. Conservatives have lost the cause to which they could rally support. From the Free Trade liberalism of an

expanding Commonwealth people have turned to the socialism which may characterize an Empire in its decline. In
twentieth-century Britain socialism has been the only creed
and the Conservatives have had to accept the greater part of
it. What they have *not* accepted is the classless society and
this is the issue on which the current conflict must inevitably
centre. For the Labour Party was committed from the beginning to the doctrine of equality, and the first practical effect
of socialism is to reduce the privileges which used to accompany wealth. Deprived of his lands and his castle, his servants
and tenants, his social and political rank, the man whose
wealth remains can use it only for personal comfort and economic power. With less motive now for effort, he can still
however seek public office. In doing so, he will perhaps have
the advantages of education, leisure, status and confidence.
But the Socialists feel that these advantages are unfair. They
believe that all should start level and that the prizes should go
to those who have earned them by their individual merit. It
is thus the theory of the classless society that all should attend
the same type of school and that the selection of the more
promising pupils should be left to the last possible moment.
The practice is somewhat different for a number of reasons.
It is now belatedly recognized, for one thing, that inequality
starts before birth and that a child's most formative years are
those between the ages of one and three. It is also apparent
that the Labour Member of Parliament has often been born
into politics, being one of the hereditary leaders of the people.
The fact, however, that equality is impossible to achieve does
not prevent its acceptance as an ideal which can at least be
approached. In this sense the aspiration is what matters.
For many people the classless society is a positive good, while
for others it represents disaster. Faced with this alternative
we are compelled to choose.

In making this choice we are seldom deciding between the
extremes of dignity and squalor. The Conservative leader
represents, on an average, the third generation of privilege;
the Labour leader, often (but not always) the first. Socialist
politicians have risen, many of them, through the ranks of a

trade-union hierarchy. Some are university graduates of middle-class origin and others, more fortunate, are the graduate sons of trade-union fathers. They point with pride to their undistinguished origin and boast sometimes of their parents' sufferings when on the Dole. The Conservative leader owes far more, by contrast, to his father and grandfather. His family legend begins with the poor boy who worked his passage, studied at nights, saved his money and ended as supervisor, technician or shopkeeper. It was his youngest son who made the family fortune and married the daughter of a judge or general. All three sons of that marriage went to Eton and Christchurch and the youngest had a commission, as well, in the Coldstream Guards. Following his marriage to the daughter of a viscount, this imaginary man of the third generation entered Parliament and reached the front bench as Chancellor of the Duchy of Lancaster. The point of such a career is that it took two generations of effort to place the future politician at the point where his own efforts could tell. There was an inherited streak of ability, the grandfather being quite as able as his descendants, and an initial urge to escape from poverty. There was the father's enterprise and energy, crossed with resolution and brains on the mother's side, and the final product – with a certain amount of wastage – was a Conservative Cabinet Minister. Is he better – as he is certainly younger – than his socialist opponent? It might be difficult, at least, to prove that he is worse.

In comparing the merits of these two ways in which leaders may be chosen, the Socialist is hampered by his sense of fairness. He feels that the third generation of a rising family has an undue advantage over the first. In the classless society this would be prevented by a system of comprehensive schools and intelligence tests. What he forgets is that fairness can hardly be an object in itself. If we depend for our light and heat on an electricity plant, our need is for a man who will make it work. That the members of the selection committee were scrupulously fair in their choice of manager is not really of much concern. 'A is good', they might have told each other, 'but B, given the same advantages, might have been just as efficient.' So he might, but the committee choose A, caring only to ensure the best results. What is true of a power plant is doubly true of the Treasury, Home Office or Ministry of Defence. That all citizens should have an equal chance of being chosen for office is a trivial matter. Our concern is to save the country from its bureaucrats, criminals and enemies. If we drift into bankruptcy, chaos or defeat, it is poor consolation to reflect that ours was once (when it existed) a classless society. To compare different forms of government by any yardstick other than that of practical results is obviously futile. That, however, is what the socialist tends to do. He begins with a textbook picture of how society should be organized and then complains that reality (whether in Spain, Portugal or South Africa) is something entirely different. Quite widely different it is likely to be, for each country is faced by a different problem. Our one certainty in these matters is that the final test is not the socialist textbook but the facts of success or failure, the fact above all of survival.

The classless society means that all are to start fairly from the lower-class level. This means that the ambitious individual is to achieve in one lifetime what has previously been spread over three generations of effort. Rejecting the example of Mr John F. Kennedy, we are to prefer the example afforded by Mr Harold Wilson. To the grandfather's grim determination we are to add (in the same life span) the father's enterprise and the son's knowledge of the world. All this is just possible (indeed it has been done), but the one life is seldom long enough. The manifest danger is of men reaching the Cabinet already spent. This has happened often enough and we shall see it happen again. The world has become more complex since the days of Abraham Lincoln, and the technological trend of the day would seem to favour the three-stage rocket. There is also some justification for the biological approach, for the supposition that breeding and heredity have a part to play. According to socialist doctrine it is laudable for a young man to say, 'I mean to be Prime Minister.' Is it so wicked for another young man to say, with greater diffi-

dence, 'I mean to make my grandson Prime Minister'?
Uncertainties surround this latter approach, for who is to say
what sort of grandson (if any) he may have? But a series of
parents who make some similar resolve should perhaps produce a winner among them. Is it so wrong to believe, as they
do, that future leaders can be bred and trained for leadership?

If it were simply a choice between these two types of leader,
the Socialist might have some mathematical grounds for
thinking the lower-class candidate the better man. He is chosen from among a million others, while his Conservative
opponent is chosen from among a thousand. That is a sufficient argument, perhaps, for voting Labour. It is not enough
to justify the plea for a classless society. For that would mean
something quite different, the elimination of all candidates
whose origin is not from the one class. Instead of advising
the citizen to vote Labour, the Socialist wants to deprive him
of any alternative. During the crisis of World War II, when
Britain's mere existence was at stake, there was room in the
leadership for Ernest Bevin and Herbert Morrison. There was
room for Aneurin Bevan and, at a slightly lower level, for
Harold Wilson. But the classless society, had it existed then,
would have had no room for Churchill or Alanbrooke, for
Alexander or Montgomery, for Cunningham or Tedder, for
Wavell or Slim. To have supplanted them all by classless
leaders might have been an advantage but this is a theory for
which we have no proof. Lacking any certainty on the subject
we may feel grateful for the leaders that we had and doubtful
of any reform which might exclude such men at any similar
crisis which may arise. If the British system of party government is based, however vaguely, on the game of cricket, we
can understand either side wanting to prolong its innings.
The Labour Party, however, wants to do more than that. It
wants to abolish the opposing side.

With the demand for the classless society goes the Socialist
attack on individual ownership, implicit in Labour Party
doctrine from the first. Demands on this subject have wavered
from time to time, but the view generally held on the Left is
that a man may own his house and garden, his furniture and

car, but should not own a factory, workshop or landed estate. Free as a consumer, he must not be free to produce. The public ownership of the means of production has thus been and is still a professed object of the Labour Party. People outside (and even inside) the movement have come to realize that public ownership is not the same thing as public control. Even if it were, however, there is good reason to think that the whole theory is wrong and that it strikes at the very root of civilization. It would be morally wrong even if it were relevant, and none the less wrong for allowing private ownership in the things produced. It would make more sense, in fact, to have private production for public use. There is an argument for communism as applied to consumer goods and even a precedent in Christian doctrine. There is no valid argument as affecting the means of production, for there what might seem morally right is practically wrong. This was pointed out long ago by Eric Gill, the Catholic sculptor and craftsman, who differed on this point from the leaders of his Church:

We have used the moral argument when it is precisely the moral argument which does not apply; or rather we have used the moral argument when it is precisely the moral argument which is against us! Man's right to private property is not primarily a moral right. It is not as a moral being that he claims ownership or can claim it. As a moral being private ownership is exactly the one thing he cannot claim. . . . It is by reason of his intellectual nature not of his morality, that man may and must make claim to individual ownership. We have in our pride sought a moral right to enjoyment where we had no such right; and we have foregone an intellectual right as workmen, where it was necessary for the good of things themselves. It is for the good of the property itself that 'as many as possible shall be encouraged to become owners.' (Pope Leo XIII.) It is as artists, in the proper and broad sense of the word as used by the philosopher, it is as responsible workmen, that men must own; for it is only as owners that they can do to things as they should be done by, and that, and that alone, is the ground upon which it is said that men tend to look after their own property better than that which is owned in common . . . while in the order of *doing*, of prudence, of service to one another, the use of things shall be in common, in the order of *making,* and for the sake of the good of the things made, ownership must be private.

Eric Gill, *Work and Property.*
Dent, London, 1937, p.105.

This is very near the truth, the argument weakened only – as regards common use – by the fact that maintenance is an extension of the original creativity.

The theory of the classless society forbids us to accept any large reward for the service we may render. We are to have no hereditary title or country estate. We are similarly forbidden to procure any significant advantage for our children. We must not control the business we have created. Neither the factory nor the things produced must bear the stamp of our personality, knowledge, taste or skill. If we retain ambition it can only be for public office. Should we not be elected or otherwise appointed, we must gear our lives to the stupidity of the folk next door. This is the democratic practice of socialism and it assumes an almost heroic virtue in all those whose ability is above the average. Denied the creative satisfaction of the landowner, they are left only with the pleasures of power, which they must never abuse and which they may not even attain. We are thus left to assume that men under a socialist regime are to be better and wiser than the men we know. We are not told how this transformation is to be brought about. We know, however, from history that sudden change is possible. Motivations can be altered but only by religion, never (so far as we know) by studies of political, social, or economic theory. Where the practice of socialism is concerned, such a religion exists and it is called Marxism. It is based on revelation and has all the known characteristics of a missionary cult. It is very formidable indeed and as remote from democracy as is the Church of Rome. The party members, the Jesuits of the twentieth century, have a strict discipline and a high sense of mission. As members of an ordained priesthood, they are different from the other people with whom we have to live and work. Realizing this, the founders of British socialism ended, many of them, as communists. They realized that the responsibility that must rest upon the socialist leader is too heavy for any but the most dedicated of men. In all common sense and honesty they ended thus in Marxism. To stop short of this, in the style of the British socialists, talking of democratic equality but dreaming of the plan which is to save the world, is merely futile. Without Marxism as its logical sequel, socialism is nothing.

SOCIALISM AND THE FUTURE

MR HAROLD WILSON claimed at Blackpool in 1965 that he and his colleagues had never lost sight of 'the great design of the structure we are seeking to build'. Like other democratic leaders, Sir Winston Churchill among them, he is eager to lead the British people 'to where they deserve to be led' – 'to a new age of fulfilment' – 'to an exciting and wonderful period in our history' – to the new Britain which the Labour Party sees itself as creating. Behind most of the speeches on either side of the House there lies the basic assumption that utopia lies ahead. Strive with renewed purpose, overcome the immediate difficulties, turn the corner and there we shall find the Promised Land. We might be tempted to conclude that all politicians have offered as much in every age but this would be untrue. The idea of Progress has not characterized every epoch, nor has it been the subject of every exhortation. Talk of the golden age to come has been a feature, generally speaking, of periods during which some further triumphs might be expected. In an age of expansion, with new horizons beckoning, some optimistic talk about the future could be fairly justified. After appalling casualties and the collapse of the Empire, the concept for us has become obsolete. If there had been a moment for building Jerusalem in England's green and pleasant land, that moment has plainly passed us by. In other countries there may be plans for reaching the moon. Our problem in Britain is one, rather, of saving what we can from the wreck.

The idea of Progress, by which Mr Wilson's thinking is influenced, dates from about the fourteenth century, until which period the western world looked back rather than forward. Just as Indians, Chinese and Greeks believed in a past Golden Age, the medieval Europeans knew of a past civilization superior to their own. The future might promise the Second Coming of Christ but it offered improvement in no other sense. Only when men drew level with their tremendous past dared they speak of the future with confidence. The publication of *Utopia* in 1516 marked the acceptance of a new idea, that the present is an improvement on the past and that the future should be better, therefore, than the present. In the light of this belief it became natural to ask what changes might be expected and whether they could be hastened or influenced by current policy. All our political theories rest upon this concept of progress. Our literature on the subject ends, by contrast, with the appearance of H. G. Wells' *Modern Utopia* of 1905.

We generally assume, then, that our civilization is being improved as well as disseminated, the horizon of the future being bathed in golden light. Revolutions and wars, inconvenient perhaps in themselves, were landmarks on the broad highway of progress. The Golden Age lay not in the past but in the future. The role of mankind was to press on towards its destiny, and few there were who dared ask why. The route lay onwards and upwards and the towers of Utopia were somewhere ahead. In this confident advance of the western world each nation had its turn of leadership. From the Italian States the torch was passed to Portugal, to Spain, to Holland, to France, to Britain and now, in the present age, to the United States, with Russia to follow as last of the western team. Each successive nation has had its period of greatness, with cultural achievement linked to a military and political ascendency. Each has had a rise, a peak of success, a decline of power and a fall to something like its original level. That leadership passed long ago from Britain is now sufficiently obvious. What is more difficult is to define the moment of highest achievement. If we list, however, the hundred men and women who are most frequently mentioned in the history book, we may find that the majority of them lived between 1750 and 1845. There is, of course, a difficulty about deciding who our greatest men have been. It is difficult to stifle all prejudice and disregard all personal preference, but there are some grounds for believing that the year 1775 represents a summit, never since equalled, and that 1845 begins the period of decline.

Had we been born in 1755 our acquaintances in 1775 (including the old and the very young) could have theoretically comprised Robert Adam, Jane Austen, Jeremy Bentham, James Boswell, Edward Burke, Robert Clive, James Cook, Thomas Erskine, Charles James Fox, Thomas Gainsborough, David Garrick, Edward Gibbon, Oliver Goldsmith, Edward Hawke, Warren Hastings, Samuel Johnson, Horatio Nelson, William Pitt (the elder), Joshua Reynolds, David Ricardo, John Scott (Lord Eldon), Walter Scott, Richard Brinsley Sheridan, Sarah Siddons, Adam Smith, James Watt, Arthur Wellesley, John Wesley, William Wilberforce and William Wordsworth. Suppose, however, that we were still alive in 1845 (aged 90) we might have mourned the death of George Byron, John Sell Cotman, John Keats and Percy Bysshe Shelley while still boasting acquaintance with Isambard Brunel, Lewis Carroll, Charles Darwin, Charles Dickens, Benjamin Disraeli, William Ewart Gladstone, Thomas Hardy, Thomas Henry Huxley, Henry Irving, Joseph Lister, David Livingstone, Thomas Babington Macaulay, John Stuart Mill, William Morris, John Henry Newman, Florence Nightingale, Cecil Rhodes, John Ruskin, Alfred Tennyson, William Thackeray, Anthony Trollope and Queen Victoria. Our parents (born in 1720) might in this case have known George Anson, Daniel Defoe, William Hogarth, Jonathan Swift and James Wolfe. With longevity matching ours, the children born to us around 1805 could have lived to see Edward Elgar, Rudyard Kipling, Winston Churchill, T. E. Lawrence, John Masefield, Alfred Milner, Ernest Rutherford, Robert F. Scott, George Bernard Shaw and H. G. Wells. It is impossible to be fair to the present age, with its potential genius still perhaps at school, but we can hardly expect to see around us the sort of talent which seems to have been available between 1750 and 1845. No one familiar with British history would expect to find it. No visitor from another country is heard to remark on it. We make no such claim for ourselves.

Of undisputed genius we had little by 1930, less by 1940 and practically none by the day of Churchill's death in 1965. Our most creative period is over and we might be justified in identifying two phases of maximum effort. During the first phase the naval and military triumphs of the Seven Years War led on to the intellectual, artistic, colonial and technological achievements which followed. During the second, the epic of the Napoleonic War was the prelude to another burst of activity — literary, industrial, imperial and scientific — which began to lose its momentum in about 1845. Arthur Wellesley, Duke of Wellington, came near to viewing both phases in the course of one tremendous lifetime. That these were the great days is surely not in question.

Although no longer leading among the western nations, Britain still shares in the sort of progress which is common to them all. Lagging a little behind the United States, just as Europe generally used to lag behind Britain, the Commonwealth boasts its own sort of progress. Our highest achievements are in the past but we can point to our current progress in two directions; first, towards technical perfection, and second, towards democracy. Material improvement is closely linked, in the early days, with intellectual ascendancy. It continues, however, after that ascendancy has been lost. For one thing, it is quantitative, the later railways being merely copies of the first. For another, it is transmissible, people being able to import what they could never invent. With foreign aid they can also import what they could not otherwise afford. Governments based upon practically illiterate populations have their own television and radio. Aircraft of identical pattern bear the brightly painted insignia of Mumbojumbo Airlines and Air Nitwitzerland. These outward and visible signs do not indicate, of necessity, an onward and spirited pace. So long, however, as the motive power is there, material progress may well continue and most probably will. After all, one hydro-electric scheme leads to another. The pressure group is in existence and the procedure has been established, another viaduct follows the last and another reservoir must follow the one we have just completed. Civil engineers need employment, just like anyone else. We cannot abandon any type of project merely because we have enough. Progress of this kind is inexorable. The team set up to ruin Ullswater will go on to ruin Windermere. Half the water obtained may be wasted through a faulty design of water-closet but any comment on this must be regarded as anti-social. Mischief cannot be halted and the trend cannot be reversed. Who are we, ask the progressives, to stand in the way of Progress?

Democracy is also regarded as a form of progress; as a move towards a loftier type of civilization. Were that the case we should have difficulty in explaining why it should be associated with a period of intellectual and artistic decline. The fact is, however, that democracy represents a merely biological trend, a phase in the political cycle. It may prove beneficial in a certain context. It may suit the technical circumstances of a given region or period. It is not, however, an end in itself; nor can it exist except as one phase of a continuing process. In Britain this process is particularly manifest, being spread over something like a thousand years. The first task was to create a national unity, necessary at first for defence and essential later in the period of expansion. This involved a spasmodic effort spread over about seven hundred years. After tremendous planning and labour, persuasion and bloodshed, it became possible (in about 1600) to draw a boundary and say, 'This is Britain – the rest is not.' The boundary included Scotland but excluded Gascony. It comprised Wales and Ireland but excluded Calais. It defined the area of the homeland or base. This, the first and most difficult task, was accomplished by the Monarchy; nor could it conceivably have been done under any other form of rule. Only a monarchy can unite for it is only a monarch that can marry. By the death of Elizabeth I, Britain, as a potential world power, had been brought into existence. Its later phase of leadership had become at least geographically possible.

Monarchy and nobility go together, abolition of one meaning abolition of both. Essential basis of the nobility (were there no other) is the royal family itself. If the Monarch's uncles, brothers and nephews are placed on a level with the populace, the throne is discredited by its associations. But the rank accorded to a dim-witted relative cannot be higher — or, anyway, much higher — than that allowed to a trusted minister or general. A nobility is thus inevitable. It must also, as inevitably, become more numerous as the centuries pass. With this growth in numbers the nobility, with its own fringe of relatives, becomes more influential as a body. By the same process the individual head of a noble family comes to matter less. He cannot rival the Monarch except as leader of a faction or pressure group. By the simplest of biological processes the nobility turns itself into an aristocracy. Widening its basis of support and rallying the gentry to its cause, the aristocracy ceases to dream of provincial revolt and begins to demand a share — and an increasing share — of the central authority. By 1700 Britain had both a ruling aristocracy and a party system. Under aristocratic leadership Britain conquered an empire and established itself as the chief naval, commercial and industrial power in Europe. The British were disciplined, inspired, ruthless and energetic as never before or since, foremost in the West at the moment when the West reached its zenith. In the wake of this tremendous achievement came the main British contributions to exploration, architecture, science and art, gardening, invention, philanthropy and sport. We look back in wonder at all our ancestors managed to do.

An aristocracy falls through the same biological process by which it rose. It becomes more numerous, its more impoverished members being assimilated into a middle class which thus adds ancestry to moderate wealth. More and more people claim the status of gentry, some individually because they are rich and others collectively because the dentist now counts as an officer. All established traditions restrict political office to gentlemen, but this ends as the word on the lavatory door. For political purposes all voters are the 'Ladies and Gentlemen' to whom the candidate addresses his speech. Where the aristocracy's reputation rests, as in Britain, on a colossal story of creative conquest, the process is slower than in a country like France which had its phase of international leadership under a monarchy. It is inexorable, nevertheless, and it is accompanied by a slackening of effort. The rewards and penalties become less impressive. Slowly – too slowly for some, too quickly for others – the country becomes a democracy. Power comes to be vested in a large number of people. They may not constitute a majority and they seldom do, but those ruling may seem fairly typical of the rest. The talk, moreover, is of an equality which has to be extended successively to the poor, the alien, the female and the adolescent. There is a dwindling difference between employers and employed, between officers and men. Promotion and dismissal lose something of their old significance. As the consensus of opinion comes to matter more, the individual comes to matter less. Power comes to be vested in larger and larger groups, to which process the logical end is the assimilation by one group of the rest. Whether the eventual victors are of the Right or the Left is immaterial to this extent that the final result is, in any case, what the dictionary defines as *Totalitarian*.

Utopian philosophers from Plato to H. G. Wells have discussed the idea of the perfect Society or State; the moment reached when we can say 'Hold it!' and keep mankind thenceforward in a sort of frozen immobility. Whether that state of affairs would be desirable may be a matter of doubt. That it is unattainable is practically certain. Such long periods as we know of apparent stability – in ancient Egypt, for example, or China – are associated with monarchy. Periods of democratic rule have all been comparatively brief and have all ended in dictatorship. Nor is it difficult to see how this must come about. To vest political power in a large number of people means the virtual elimination of the minority groups between which power was formerly divided; royalty, nobility, gentry, universities, church, big business, army and law. The functions of all these groups have to be performed, thenceforward, by the democratic State. All the dignity of kingship, all the glamour of nobility, all the influence of the gentlefolk, all the inspiration of religion, all the vision of great enterprise, all daring leadership and all judicial impartiality is now demanded of the same people at the same time. As a rivalry between different kings and generals has become technically impossible, the result is that momentarily effective rule which we describe as dictatorship. As this cannot last for long – depending as it does on the lives of very mortal men – it has to be replaced by monarchy. This completes the circle and we can begin again.

From a study of British History we might be tempted to conclude that aristocracy is the best form of government. It was the form under which we triumphed, as much in the arts as in battle. We might be tempted to regard democracy as itself a sign of decay, being coincident in Britain with much that we might regard as decadent. But a wider knowledge of history must lead us to a different conclusion. Periods of leadership may coincide, it would seem, with almost any form of government, democracy included. There can be little doubt, for example, that the most creative period in the history of the United States will have been democratic. The tendency towards dictatorship is already apparent under President L. B. Johnson, while the later trend towards monarchy has been foreshadowed by Presidents Roosevelt and Kennedy. It seems virtually certain, however, that the coming dictatorship will accompany, without causing, the end of American leadership of the West. We cannot readily associate periods of national ascendancy with any particular form of rule. But neither can we regard these political changes as so many steps towards political perfection. Failing some basic change in the conditions under which we have to work, political progress must remain a myth. It is true that a democratic society can be made more egalitarian, but this hastening of the process merely shortens the life of the democracy, making dictatorship the more imminent. The theory that freedom broadens down from precedent to precedent has no basis in historical example. The pursuit of democracy does not end in perfection but in that chaos from which dictatorship offers the only means of escape. No form of government can last for ever, and democracy does not even, in practice, last for long.

The illusion of political progress is enshrined in the legend of the Bad Old Days. Through the medium of the school history book, we look back on a past in which madly tyrannical kings gave place to lawless barons and despotic squires, all replaced finally by the quiet marchinations of the Urban District Council. From Richard III to Richard Dimbleby would seem to represent a sort of progress. Granted that this is so, we have to realize that the Bad Old Days were essential to all that has followed. Without the monarchy there could have been no nation. Without the bad barons there could have been no parliament. Without the squire there could have been no bench of magistrates. None of the reforms of parliament which curbed the aristocracy would have been possible without the parliament being there to reform. None of the executive powers now vested in the Prime Minister could have been his without their previous concentration under the authority of the Crown. The competence and honesty we expect of the civil service is something that remains of its exclusive tradition – not something created by the success of our primary schools. That our armed services keep out of politics is not the result of democratic theory but of aristocratic practice. It is folly, therefore, to regard the Bad Old Days as a nightmare from which we would have been aroused. Whether bad or not, they were essential to all we now regard as valuable and progressive. This fact we rediscover each time we confer representative government on a colonial territory which has not passed through the stages of kingship and aristocracy. Everything may be there from the mace on the table to the wig on the Speaker's head, but all pretence of democracy is lost in a matter not of years but of weeks. Observing the chaos which is apt to result we often blame each other for knowing so little about the country we are trying to liberate. Our real fault is in knowing so little about the country in which we live.

If cultural and political progress is merely a delusion, material progress remains a fact. But here again we should be wrong to reject the past with horror. For progress in this sense – the sort of progress which people mostly discuss – consists in demanding that what the rich had yesterday the poor shall have tomorrow. 'In the Bad Old Days,' we are told, 'the well-to-do kept all the good things to themselves. Nowadays, we have them too.' Whether this process is invariably beneficial might often seem dubious, but even the most innocent of pleasures must be invented before it can be shared. The seaside holiday was the invention of George III, bequeathed to the Victorian gentry and middle class and finally inherited by the people at large. People do not discover this sort of luxury for themselves and many a populace has failed to discover it at all. Beds have evolved from straw to feathers and from feathers to box-spring via horse-hair, all by the process of the poor following the rich. That the rest of us are indebted to the wealthy for our ideas of comfort is proved, incidentally, by the fashion or caprice which ends as a by-law. The Victorian bathroom is bequeathed to the council house, which would have had a shower instead had that been what the Victorian gentry preferred.

All pleasures, even the most elemental, are thus pioneered (or at least elaborated) by the wealthy. They perform this service for normally selfish reasons, but the philanthropic among them, seeking to benefit mankind, follow what is essentially the same path. On the one hand the bicycle – the toy, to begin with, of the well-to-do – ends as a convenience for the errand-boy. On the other hand, the benevolent vicar's wife teaches the parishioners to play the once aristocratic game of whist. Progress in education consists in making the elementary school look like the grammar school which is trying to look like a public school. All schools end, therefore, with housemasters, prefects, blazers and caps. Progress in sport involves covering the world with imitations of Ascot, Wimbledon, Zermatt, Henley, Gleneagles, Badminton and Rugby. Progress in amenity leaves each city with parks inherited from the country house, complete with lake, tennis courts and the Edwardian sand-pit. Progress in housing gives the council house the garden-fronted semi-detachment which was once the symbol of middle-class seclusion. As seen from above, all progress means essentially 'more people like ourselves'. As seen from below, all progress means 'more of what we were previously denied'. In this limited sense progress can be regarded as real.

We may doubt, perhaps, whether material progress can continue indefinitely, or whether it would add anything to happiness if it did. But it remains true, in the meanwhile, that it depends for its future on the existence of the rich. This is still true of countries where the wealthy have been eliminated, and true even of countries where wealth has never been seen. Ideas of luxury derive, in these instances, from the motion picture or illustrated magazine. If the film actress has a tiled swimming pool there is a demand for backyard plastics from Hanbury to Odessa. If the film actor wears pyjamas these become saleable from Dubrovnik to Murmansk. That progress on these lines has done something for cleanliness and hygiene, for comfort and health, is not to be denied. That it can do mischief in other ways is at least highly probable. But the fact needs emphasis that the end of privilege must bring this sort of progress to a halt. We cannot imitate the luxury of people whose lives are no longer luxurious. We can find few new sources of pleasure if all the prosperous pleasure-seekers have been put to work in the factory. It remains true, moreover, that the quest for material progress is something which the rich and poor have in common. What the idle millionaire wants to relieve his boredom — a yacht, a pair of skis, a tropical beach or a slimming diet — becomes the birthright in time of everyone else. For the majority of people progress means little more than the sequence by which the luxuries of the rich end as the necessities of the poor. We find ourselves wondering, however, whether it will continue and whether it can represent improvement. It conflicts at the outset with all ideas of democratic equality, depending as it does on the class distinctions which our statesmen want to abolish. It also seems to foreshadow a future in which indigestion and insomnia, hypochondria and hysterics would appear, at first sight, to play too large a part. Without pleasure-seekers no new pleasure can be found. It is a question, however, whether the more satisfying pleasures are of this material kind. Could the truth be that progress (at least for twentieth-century Britain) is a delusion? If so, we might be well advised to call off the quest. Rather than strain towards the problematic future, we might do better to save something of our astonishing past. The case for real conservatism is no more (and no less) than that.

What remains, meanwhile, of socialism? The Labour Party had its first taste of power, after thirteen years, in 1964. All its measures for the next twelve months were based on ideas dating from the nineteenth century. Central to the Party's eloquence was the National Plan, the aim of which was to produce a twenty-five per cent growth in national output over the next five years. Background to the Plan, were the usual increases in taxation, the usual expansion of the civil service, the usual reductions in military strength and the usual expenditure on the welfare of the working class. All the talk in the corridors of power was of economic resources, the balance of payments, industrial efficiency and public finance. With the details we need not concern ourselves, for they, and the Plan itself, will all be forgotten before the five years have passed. Two significant facts emerge, however, and require our comment. In the first place, all this discussion of economic doctrine reveals a basic refusal to face the political facts. The world situation has changed since the period from which the Labour Party draws its inspiration. The renascence of the Far East has put a term to western ascendancy. The leadership of the West is itself in dispute, and the assassination of President Kennedy is a reminder to us that Julius Caesar's murder was preliminary to his nephew becoming Emperor. In matters scientific the lead enjoyed by U.S.A. is diminishing. The situation of western Europe has changed even more dramatically, its period of expansion finished and a new era beginning in which the emphasis must be on unity for purposes of defence. Britain's situation has changed in still more drastic fashion, reversing policies which go back to the year 1200. For strategic purposes Britain has ceased to be an island, with political consequences which people are slow to grasp. The British Empire has disintegrated under American pressure and Britain's economy has been shattered in the process. Amidst these momentous changes the Labour Party clings to its programme of 1917, its philosophy of 1894. It has learnt nothing, forgotten nothing in the course of fifty years.

What are the actual and urgent problems which face Britain today? The first is to disengage the country from what remains of its Empire, while retaining the proud memory of all that was achieved. The socialist's instinct is to cling to the useless encumbrance while smearing the historic reputation. The second problem is to prepare Britain for the part it must play in a United States of Europe. This has become a strategic and political necessity but the immediate need is not for argument with France but for a re-organization of Britain. The move must be away from nationalism, but the socialist's instinct is always to nationalize. The implications of what we must attempt are beyond the limited imagination of the men we have elected. Our third and obvious problem concerns our whole machinery of government. Visiting Vienna we recognize it at once as the capital of an empire that no longer exists. Returning to London, we fail to recognize its similarity. Our whole structure of politics was designed in different circumstances for the solution of different problems. The crying need is for political reform, a regrouping of forces to meet an entirely new situation. But the socialists have never had any political theory of any kind. Behind them, in all its impressive immensity, there looms an intellectual vacuum.

The second significant fact about the Labour Party's policy and Plan is that the earlier enthusiasm for state ownership is no longer so obvious. More industrial plants are to be nationalized but nobody sees in this a clue to prosperity. Most of the socialists have tacitly agreed, moreover, that much of industry must be left to private enterprise. They envisage, therefore, a dual economy in which the public and private sectors are to co-exist under the protection of a benevolently neutral government. But how is this compatible with a belief that all capitalists are wicked? How can there be a friendly partnership or even a sporting rivalry between those whose ideals are known to be enlightened and those whose motives are known to be base? In Mr Wilson's opinion, Conservative industrialists belong to a closed society 'in which birth and wealth have priority'. This is a society which the Labour Party leaders would like to destroy, down to and including the schools at which the Conservatives were educated. But how is this consistent with co-operation round the conference table and the pooling of ideas to be contributed by management, trade unions and civil service? Some co-operation there must be but socialist oratory does little, one would judge, to improve the cordiality of the discussion. Mr Wilson wants to negotiate agreements today with men whose throats he will cut tomorrow. There is nothing very admirable in these tactics, nor is there any reason for supposing that they can succeed. Some industrialists are admittedly stupid, but few, surely, are as stupid as that.

With the General Election of 1966 the Labour Party returned to office with greater assurance, their majority strengthened and their mandate approved. That the Party should have been re-elected was in no way surprising, for its turn for office had come. Voters with no particular love for socialism were bound to feel, as many did, that the Conservatives had been in power for quite long enough. Others felt that the Socialists, like the Liberals of fifty years before, had carried out their original plans and had been unable to find any others. It was only fair, even so, to give them a chance, and this is the chance they have. Faced by urgent and complex problems of the day Mr Wilson is often astute. Where he fails is in restoring what the country needs above all, a sense of national purpose. He is ready to make war on want and do all he can to promote the happiness of the common man. But mere happiness must never be the main object of life. It is, like peace, a by-product; something achieved incidentally by people whose quest is for justice. Under a great leader, champion of a great cause, social inequalities and hardships are not abolished but they are forgotten. A great cause must be external, however, to ourselves. A campaign merely to abolish poverty and want must make people more, not less, aware of their own rights and grievances; less, not more, aware of their duties and their chance to serve. Its failure is implicit in the very nature of its appeal. Mr Wilson would like to see a society in which every citizen has regular employment with good pay, a good house with all modern conveniences, a good train service between suburb and factory, a reliable supply of electricity and water, an enlightened school for his children (not manifestly inferior to any other school), an efficient health service, a car for use at the weekends and leisure in which to attend evening classes or stand for election to the Urban District Council. If asked what the next step is to be, he would possibly mutter something about Culture and the Arts, about Comradeship, World Peace and (conceivably) God. An inevitable comment on this sequence of thought is that these ultimate aims – if they are the right ones – should have been considered first, taking precedence over the gas-cooker and the omnibus. But it is more immediately relevant to say that the society Mr Wilson wants to see is already in existence. He can see it whenever he feels the urge. Over large parts of the United States the perfect life, in this sense, has been already achieved. Poverty may exist in some areas and squalor is not unknown, but the middle-class suburb is more the rule than the exception. The American Way of Life is less socialist than Mr Wilson can approve, but far more socialist than the Americans themselves will admit. Whatever the inequalities and whatever the injustices, vast areas of suburban prosperity have come into existence; and the continued existence of an occasional millionaire or slum does not affect our comment on the suburbs themselves. They fairly represent a people's success in the search for material comfort, education, leisure and health. They are all that the Labour Party could possibly offer, and far more than the Labour Party is likely to provide.

And what is the result? After the first generation the result is boredom. The effect on the young is symbolized by the disorders which occur on occasion at the University of California, Berkeley Campus. The effect of (relative) prosperity on the Negroes was demonstrated in the Los Angeles Riots. The roots of the problem were explained long ago in *West Side Story* — told within the context of a well-fed and well-clothed adolescence. And here in Britain the same symptoms of unrest are apparent in a society not yet half as prosperous. Crimes that are committed in growing number are not the crimes of poverty but of affluence. The criminals are sometimes men whose enterprise has had no other outlet. Juvenile crime, increasing yearly, is not caused by any lack of schooling but specifically by a schooling which is too prolonged. A wave of drug-addiction and gambling is due to boredom, not to unemployment. The utopia built on wage-packets, dental clinics and dishwashers begins to fall apart before it has been completed. For while a world of social security has something to recommend it to the middle-aged, it offers little, by contrast, to the Mods and Rockers, the Beatniks and Crooners. For the young of any period in history, the quest for comfort is not enough.

It is against this background of discontent that the Socialists make their Edwardian plea for social justice. Given a crime wave their only remedy is more policemen. For juvenile delinquency their only remedy is a longer period in school. They deplore the materialism of the Conservative, who still regards the profit motive as the mainspring of an industrial society. What they fail to see is that trade union motivation is just as material and no more virtuous. So far indeed as materialism goes, the Socialists and Conservatives are not only both mistaken but they make, in effect, the same mistake. In the programme which is to guide us for the rest of the century, the chief object should be neither wages nor dividends but an over-riding national purpose; one for which people might be willing to give their lives. The future lies with the Party that can point the way, not back to the dream of Beatrice and Sidney Webb but forward to the world in which we shall have to live. Which Party is it to be?

THE CO-OPERATIVE MOVEMENT

IT is suggested in Chapter 5, that the Trade Unions fail through their lack of any aim external to their members' welfare. It might be argued that the Co-operative Movement began with a higher sense of mission and should, in theory, have had a greater influence. It is apparent, however, that the Co-operative Societies soon lose sight of their original ideals. Their efforts on behalf of education and culture mostly died out long ago. All that remains would seem to consist of the Co-operative College with its rival at Loughborough and its offshoot at Wilmslow. If the Co-operative movement is to persist in its declared aim of establishing the Co-operative Commonwealth, this College might be the intellectual headquarters from which the campaign might be directed. That it is nothing of the kind is apparent from the total sums voted for educational purposes. The Societies seem to devote ½ per cent of their funds to education, or about 6½d. per member per year. But much of this reckless expenditure goes on administration, propaganda and social meetings; and much again on Youth Clubs, Pathfinders Circles and Rainbow Playways Groups. Out of what remains the College is financed, doing little more than offer technical instruction to selected shop assistants, factory hands and clerks. These have mostly been given scholarships, enabling them to take a diploma in social, secretarial or managerial studies. Aged about 28, on an average, they return better qualified and with renewed inspiration to the Societies from which they came. Of the teachers at the College an increasing number, we learn, are university graduates. As the 1953–4 enrolment came to a total of 103, we can fairly regard this as an educational enterprise in which money is no object, and where only the best will do. As a base, however, from which to conquer the world, it falls short, perhaps, of the Jesuit ideal. It illustrates, rather, the sharp contrast which exists between Co-op theory and practice. The Consumers' Democracy, in which the managers are chosen by the customers' elected representatives, is about as real as the equally democratic Company in which the directors are elected by the shareholders. It is notorious, in fact, that Co-op meetings are ill-attended, that many of those present turn out to be employees, and that the committee members virtually appoint each other. In 1963 a survey established the fact that 0.17 per cent of the membership attended meetings and 0.95 per cent took the trouble to vote. So far as from being a band of starry-eyed idealists, the Co-op members are merely folk who want their groceries cheap.

It is logical to ask at this point whether Co-op prices are in fact lower than those marked elsewhere in the High Street. During the nineteenth century they certainly must have been, but the rise of the multiple chain store has faced the C.W.S. with a more formidable type of competition. The difference in prices between the different types of store is in fact surprisingly small – something of the order of 5 per cent. An independent survey, however, conducted in 1961, revealed that a typical London family's shopping basket cost £2 12s. 5½d. at the average independent grocers, £2 10s. 6¾d at the multiple store and £2 11s. 8d. at the Co-operative Stores. Payment of the dividend would bring the Co-op price down to £2 10s. 5¾d., fractionally below the multiple store price, but substantially the same. If the independent grocer is sometimes as much as 5 per cent dearer, this difference may be covered in some instances by economies in time and transport; the shop round the corner being within walking distance and the trip to the High Street absorbing a part of the 2s. 5¾d. weekly that is theoretically saved. A rough price check in 1965 gave the London Co-operative Stores a marginal advantage over the Supermarket in eggs, cheese, coffee, bananas and apples, while it proved fractionally more expensive to purchasers of 'Tide' soap powder and stewing steak. A check on hardware prices revealed that the Co-op was slightly cheaper for tablecloths, forks and teaspoons, slightly dearer for crockery and much dearer for plastic items, frying-pans, glassware and lamp bulbs. But comparisons are difficult, partly because there are differences between one Co-operative Society and another and partly because hardware items can be thought to differ in quality and design.

Generally speaking the Co-operative Societies do best with goods which are in steady demand, like milk and bread, and worst with clothing and semi-luxury items. They are most attractive to middle-aged customers, as was shown in a survey made in 1960, 40 per cent of their members being 55 or more and only 17 per cent under 35. They are least attractive to young women, and scarcely more so to teenage youths. Seeing their typical customer as a 45-year-old working-class woman, living in the North of England, the Co-ops have retained their 'cloth-cap' image, doing little to cater for the young and frivolous. The accent in men's clothes is on low price and value for money but the women's clothes are often expensive and dowdy, with too narrow a range and too little regard for the fashion of the day. Many of the shops themselves have been modernized but they remain the sort of place where a girl might buy her jeans but not her dance frock. To shop at the Co-op is too sensible to be interesting, the marginal economies being offset by a lack of adventure. There is little evidence that Co-operative customers are aware of the ideals upon which the Co-operative Movement is supposed to be based. All that reaches them of the doctrine of brotherhood is the drab atmosphere in which it was first proclaimed. Something of Toad Lane, Rochdale, has survived, gaining the approval of some but equally earning the dislike of those whose tastes are less prosaic. Considered as a whole, the Co-operative Movement is scarcely holding its own. In so far, moreover, as it seeks to modernize itself, it drifts further from its original purpose. The Co-op could end as a multiple store, pretty much like the rest.

Where does it fail? It lacks to begin with any firm direction from the top. Its democratic structure, bogus in many ways, is yet real enough as an obstacle to progress. The eight hundred Societies can pull in as many different directions.

There is little chance of mobilizing resources to exploit a success or stave off a danger. The fact, moreover, that the C.W.S. is obliged to sell the products of its own factories must place it at a disadvantage, more especially as those factories are not in competition with others. The directors of a multiple chainstore organization can play off their suppliers against each other, ensuring that no one has a secure monopoly in a given range. It is part, moreover, of the Co-op tradition that Co-op managers should be offered only the most niggardly salary. Considering this mean policy and the fact that the Manager is subject to an interfering lay committee of dedicated but unrepresentative nonentities, it is astonishing that the management is as competent as it is. But the competence is of a rather limited kind, the hallmark of people who have risen within the one organization and need not fear the sort of blood transfusion which may enliven the ordinary firm. In advertising and public relations, the views of the elderly committee members are apt to be seriously outdated and hopelessly parochial. No one can deny that the Co-op movement has benefited consumers in the past. Few would question that there is room for it in the future. But its efficiency depends upon the competition it has to meet from private enterprise. Without that spur the Co-operative retail stores would be even duller than they are.

There is some reason to think that the Co-operative movement has long since passed its zenith – perhaps as long ago as 1946. Its increase in membership has slowed down since then, tending in some areas to dwindle. Still more important, the average expenditure per member fell by one sixth (in real values) between 1940 and 1960 – being proportionately far less than was spent in 1880. Shareholding is as much on the decline and dividends have sunk, in many instances, to vanishing point; to 1 ½d. in the £, for example, at Liverpool. The result has been a sporadic attempt to modernize. Some Societies have abolished the dividend altogether, claiming to have cut their prices by an equivalent amount. Others pay 'instant dividend' in the form of vouchers which can be used in making a further purchase; not to be confused, apparently, with the wicked practice of giving 'trading stamps'. There are attempts to offer credit terms, much against the movement's tradition. There was, finally, the Gaitskell Commission, set up in 1955, which reported its critical findings in 1958. All these activities reflect the anxieties felt about the Co-op's future. But each 'streamlining' effort leads, inevitably, to a loss of identity. To correct the weaknesses of the Co-operative Stores would make their existence even more of an anomaly. Centralization of authority, following the recent reorganization of the Wholesale side, would give the movement what it clearly needs; a Dr Beeching, drawn from outside the movement. He would divorce production from distribution, telling the C.W.S. factories to sell on the open market and allowing the Co-op retailers to seek the best goods at the lowest price. Managers given wider responsibilities would expect higher salaries and would earn them. Directors, still more highly paid, would appoint new Managers, stolen from Woolworth's or Marks & Spencer's, and the advertising and window displays would become more aggressive overnight. Recognizing that the customer votes through the cash register, not at an Annual General Meeting, the Board would abolish all the elected committees and make the staff responsible to Head Office. Funds now allocated to education would be spent in future on propaganda and public relations. All the less remunerative stores would be closed, all the more successful enlarged. There would then arise the question of a new name for the Group, one suitable to the age in which we live. We might end with Co-optimist Supermarkets well known for their Co-Pop Group (The Pathfinders) on I.T.V. and almost as famous for their emphasis in advertisement on snobbery, violence and sex.

Is this an absurd exaggeration? Far from that, the trend is already manifest. When the C.W.S. tried recently to recapture some of the shoe business the Society had lost to Charles Clore, it was through a subsidiary called (of all things) Society Footwear. What is significant about this is not the policy but the name. The word 'Society' could refer, of course, to the C.W.S. itself. To the customer, however, it suggests something different. The shoes are of the sort (it is hinted) that are worn in *high society*. Shoes designed originally for Princess Margaret, Grace Kelly or Baroness Thyssen are now available to a few selected customers at the Co-op. The publicity slant is familiar enough, but what has all this to do with Toad Lane, Rochdale, the Bethlehem of Co-operation? Those directing a movement originally and defiantly working-class have already discovered that they shut themselves out of more than half the market if they fail to appeal also to youth. As compared with the Labour Party's traditional supporters, the young of today are extravagant, romantic, fashion-conscious and impulsive. Appealing to them must mean a complete revolution in outlook. The cloth-cap image has to go. Working-class no longer, the Co-op customers are on the fringe, as they dream, of Society. They have to be treated, when in that mood, as ladies and gentlemen. With that realization the whole penny-saving structure of Co-operation crashes to the ground. The Co-op is thenceforward in business like everyone else.

Two differences, however, remain. First, the wicked capitalist has been excluded, and second, there may be some advantage in legal status. To take the first point it is perfectly true that the Co-op member is contributing nothing to the comfort of the idle rich, nor even towards providing the status symbols of a well-paid management. It is true again that the multiple store may have to provide a large income for its owners and managers. This being so, it seems odd that price levels in Co-operative and privately-owned stores should be so nearly level. One is driven to the paradoxical conclusion that the capitalists must earn what they are paid or that the Co-operatives must waste on democracy what they have saved in directors' fees. It is the sad fact that economies in top-level remuneration yield more of an emotional than a financial return. The percentage theoretically saved is insignificant. The opportunities thrown away may be immense. Any first-class director or manager can save his company far more than he is paid (whatever he is paid). Given a vast organization, centrally controlled, the policy decisions become so important that the cost of making them becomes irrelevant. At this level the director is like the leading barrister whose high fee is a negligible percentage of the sum which his case may involve. By excluding the wicked capitalist, the Co-operative Stores have fatally narrowed their field of enterprise.

As regards their legal status, the British Co-operative Societies still have the advantage of being able to pay a tax-free dividend, but this has ceased to have any great significance, and their avoidance of profits tax was ended by the Finance Act of 1958. Tax advantages are far more important, however, in countries where Farming Co-operatives exist on a large scale; in U.S.A. and Canada, in Scandinavia and Holland. Everywhere we find giant middle-class organizations enjoying a tax-concession devised for poor artisans practising self-help in a back street. Of the 500 largest corporations in U.S.A. (1964) five are Farmers' Co-operatives, the largest with sales of $229,051,000. United States Farmer Co-operatives number over 9,000, with a membership of over 7 million. In Canada the Co-operatives are relatively even more important, their tax advantages being greater still. One Society with net profits of $7,690,000 in 1963 paid only $293,000 in income tax; a mere 3.80 per cent as compared with the 52 per cent to which an ordinary company is liable. Canadian Co-operatives are tending, in fact, to drive other firms out of business, merely on the basis of tax avoidance. Agricultural Co-operatives are as privileged in France and scarcely less so in Holland. They have been even more fortunate, however, in Denmark and Norway. The Danish Agricultural Co-operatives numbered over 7,000 in 1957 with a membership of 2.2 million out of a total population of about 5 million. The tax question there was been the subject of public controversy, but the Co-operatives have succeeded in retaining an advantage. The Danes are also bringing about a merger of all their consumer co-operatives, thus creating a single retail chain catering for 600,000 families. In Norway they have been successful in arguing that Co-operatives are also exempt from registration and stamp taxes.

The idea that a Co-operative is virtuous by definition has gained a wide acceptance throughout the world. The facts, however, are otherwise; ownership being of marginal importance and both private and Co-operative enterprise having come under much the same sort of professional management. In so far as the British Co-operative Societies carry their old brand image they can retain only a dwindling share of the market. In so far as they modernize, they lose the whole point of their existence. Without the tax advantages which explain co-operative successes elsewhere, the British movement is faced by this dilemma. Campaigning in what was once the right country, our co-operators find themselves in the wrong century.

APPENDIX B

THE LEFT BOOK CLUB

THE intellectual life of the British Labour Party is fairly represented by the story of the Left Book Club. This was founded by Victor Gollancz in 1936 and reached its maximum membership of 60,000 in the following year. Some sixteen hundred discussion groups were organized and there was even a rally in the Albert Hall. Victor Gollancz (1893–1967) was a humanitarian Jew of great energy who had been managing director of Benn's, the publishing house which pioneered the sixpenny paperback. He founded his own firm in 1928 and had an immediate success with *Journey's End* by R. C. Sherriff. His aim in founding the Left Book Club was to make a synthesis of socialist ideas, create a Popular Front and 'stop Hitler without war'. Books published for the Club numbered about 247 in all, the first, *Out of the Night,* appearing in 1936 and the last in 1948. The volumes were accompanied and explained in a monthly periodical called *Left News* which flourished over the same period. Authors who contributed to the series included Sir Richard Acland, Clement Attlee, Emile Burns, A. Fenner Brockway, G. D. H. and M. I. Cole, Sir Stafford Cripps, Victor Gollancz himself, J. B. S. Haldane, Harold Laski, Philip Noel-Baker, George Orwell, R. Palme Dutt, Stephen Spender, S. Swingler and R. H. Tawney. The books published were mainly concerned with immediate events and have had little circulation in later years. George Orwell's book, *The Road to Wigan Pier* (1937), is perhaps the only Left Book Club work to be classed as a work of literature. The most prolific author in this series was John Strachey, with seven titles, next to him G. D. H. Cole with six and Victor Gollancz himself with four.

Faithfully reflecting the mood of the period, the Left Book

Club publications are weakest in political theory. Readers were assumed (no doubt rightly) to be members of the Labour Party, loyal to the Webbs and needing no argument to sustain their faith. Socialist theory was thus represented by *An Outline of Political Thought* (1939) by S. Swingler, *The Acquisitive Society* (1937) by R. H. Tawney, and three works by John Strachey, *Theory and Practice of Socialism* (1936), *Federalism or Socialism?* (1940) and *Programme for Progress* (1940). After F. Allen had asked *Can Capitalism Last?* (1938) and after Stephen Spender had sounded the call *Forward from Liberalism* (1937), the socialist message came to an end. That, however, was where the Marxists began, for six of the publications deal with Marxism; one by Emile Burns, one by G. D. H. Cole and a third comparing Marx with Freud. Fourteen volumes in the series deal with Soviet Russia and another six with China, these last including *Red Star over China* (1937) by Edgar Snow and *The Chinese Communists* (1946) by Stuart Golder. One way and another, the Communist point of view is fully represented, finding some further expression in another seven books about the Spanish Civil War. But the Popular Front was to include the workers as well as the Communists. There are thus several books about Trade Unionism and one on the Co-operative Movement. More emphasis is given, however, to particular grievances, as *Six Men of Dorset* (1937) or to studies in the problems of unemployment. Most significant of these was Ellen Wilkinson's book about Jarrow, *The Town That Was Murdered* (1939). More telling still, however, were some of the attacks on Conservatism such as that implied in *Tory M.P.* (1939) by Simon Haxey. For the workers, again, there were included about twenty merely educational books, their subject matter ranging from eugenics to birth control, from chemistry to economic botany. For relaxation, finally, there were *Poems of Freedom* (1938) and the *Left Song Book* (1938).

Less fortunate was the campaign to 'stop Hitler without war'. Books on foreign countries and foreign policy form, it is true, the most numerous section in the list. Countries discussed include Austria, Czechoslovakia, Denmark, France, Greece, Eire and Poland. The country least mentioned is the U.S.A. Books denouncing the Nazi and Fascist movements number about twenty and include such titles as *Hitler the Pawn* (1936) by Rudolf Olden and *Under the Axe of Fascism* (1936) by Gaetano Salvemini. Denunciations came most loudly, however, from avowed pacifists whom any dictator could safely ignore. Book titles range from *Battle for Peace* (1938) by F. Elwyn Jones to *Struggle for Peace* (1936) by Sir Stafford Cripps. Victor Gollancz himself asked *Is Mr Chamberlain Saving the Peace?* (1939) and Leonard Woolf complained of *Barbarians at the Gate* (1939). The note of pessimism in *Why Capitalism Means War* (1938) by H. N. Brailsford was answered confidently by Eleanor Rathbone whose conclusion was that *War Can Be Averted* (1938). All this drivel was definitely harmful to British interests as well as to the cause (for what it was worth) of peace. An odd sequel was the Left Book Club contribution to civil defence; *A.R.P.* (1938) by J. B. S. Haldane, *Protection of the Public from Aerial Attack* (1937) by a group of Cambridge scientists, and *How to be Safe from Air Raids* (1938) by J. B. S. Haldane again. These publications reveal the general attitude of the Left towards international affairs. First, the country should disarm in the cause of peace, reducing the armed forces to a minimum and undermining the morale of the troops by assuring them that wars are caused by capitalists and arms manufacturers. Second, we should proclaim our undying opposition to the Nazi and Fascist movements in Germany and Italy. Third, we should interfere in the Spanish Civil War, supporting the 'government' against 'the rebels'. Fourth, we should strive above all *For Peace and Friendship* (1937) and, fifth, we should concentrate our main effort not on winning the coming war but on saving the civilian population from air attack. This was the road to Munich, if not to Wigan Pier.

Towards the Commonwealth the attitude of the Left was indicated, first of all, by Alexander Campbell's book, *It's Your Empire* (1945). A certain responsibility was thus assumed but the books on this topic reveal a lack of interest. *Empire or Democracy* by L. Barnes (1939) defines an alternative and *Subject India* (1943) by H. N. Brailsford suggests an attitude. Two other books about India with *Left Turn Canada* (1946) by M. J. Coldwell, and *When Smuts Goes* (1948) by Arthur Keppel-Jones, go to complete the Left Book Club's survey of the Dominions. The colonies are dealt with in one general work, *Colour, Race and Empire* (1944) by A. G. Russell and two books about Africa; one of them, by John Burgen, entitled *Black Man's Burden* (1943). Little interest was shown in Australia or New Zealand, in Malaya or the West Indies, and practically none in the Middle East except as illustrating the Jewish Question.

Left Book Club publications were priced at 2s. 6d. each, implying a fairly large circulation. Membership remained sufficient, however, during World War II and up to the time of the General Election of 1945. With Labour in power, membership dwindled rapidly and stood at just over 3,000 when the Club's activities were brought to an end in 1948. The last volumes incurred a considerable loss and Victor Gollancz went on to campaign in other directions. What is particularly interesting about this story is the fact that the Left Book Club provided only the literature of criticism and revolt. The basic ideas dated from before World War I and each current problem was seen in the light of an accepted creed. Books in this series had a limited range of mythology and grievance, exhortation and attack. Without a Conservative government, the whole movement died away. It might, of course, be argued that the Club, by 1945, had served its purpose. This was true in a negative sense but the formation of a Labour government should in theory have led to an outburst of creative thinking. *Labour's Plan for Plenty* by Michael Young came in 1947 and the electoral triumph of 1945 should have heralded a spate of even more constructive proposals. The energies which had been absorbed in warfare were free now to build Jerusalem in Britain's green and pleasant land. Intellectually, however, the Labour Party had long since shot its bolt. The Left Book Club series tailed away with duller books and fewer readers. Even a further and prolonged period in opposition failed to revive the Club, which is now no more than a memory.

If *Out of the Night* (1936) by H. J. Muller marked the beginning of this series, we can see an equal significance in the titles with which it came to an end, namely *Prisoners of Fear* (May 1948), *How Long the Night* (August 1948) and, last of all, *The Meaning of Marxism* (November 1948).

BIBLIOGRAPHY

ALLEN, Frederick, *Can Capitalism Last?* London, 1938.

ANGELL, Sir Norman, *The Steep Places.* London, 1947.

ATTLEE, Rt Hon. Clement Richard (1st. Earl Attlee), *The Labour Party in Perspective.* London, 1937 (new ed.).

BAILEY, J., *The British Co-Operative Movement.* London, 1955.

BARNES, Leonard, *Empire or Democracy?* London, 1939.

BARON, N., *British Trade Unions.* London, 1947.

The Co-Operative Movement in Labour Britain. London, 1943.

BEACONSFIELD, First Earl of, *see under* Disraeli.

BEVAN, Aneurin, *In Place of Fear.* London, 1952.

BLAIR, Eric, *see under* Orwell, George.

BOLINGBROKE, 1st Viscount, St John Henry, *Dissertation on Parties.* London, 1730.

BRAUNTHAL, Julius, *In Search of the Millennium,* London, 1945.

BRIGGS, Asa, and John Saville, *Essays in Labour History in memory of G. D. H. Cole,* London. 1960.

BROCKWAY, Fenner, *Inside the Left: a political autobiography.* London, 1942.

Socialism over sixty years: The Life of Jowett of Bradford, (1864–1944). London, 1946.

BROGAN, Colm, *Fifty years on.* London, 1950.

BROGAN, Sir Denis (William), *The Price of Revolution.* London, 1951.

BURNS, Emile, *Handbook of Marxism.* London, 1935.

What is Marxism? London, 1950.

CALDER, Nigel, *The Revolutionary in the White Coat.*

CAMBRAY, P. G., *The Game of Politics.* London, 1932.

CARPENTER, Edward, *Forecast of the coming century.* London, 1897.

CATO, *Guilty Men.* London, 1940

CHESTERTON, G. K., *George Bernard Shaw.* London, 1909 (new ed. 1935).

What's wrong with the World. London, 1912.

CLYNES, Rt Hon. John Robert, *Memoirs, 1869–1924.* London, 1937.

COLE, G. D. H., *A Century of Co-operation.* Manchester 1945.

Meaning of Marxism. London, 1948.

Means of Full employment. London, 1943.

Simple Case for Socialism. London, 1935.

William Morris, Centenary Edition. London, 1934.

The World of Labour. London, 1913.

COLE, Margaret Isabel, *The Webbs and their work.* London, 1949.

CONNELL, John Henry Robertson, *Death on the Left.* London, 1958.

The Moral Decline of the Labour Party. London, 1958.

CRANE, Peggy, 'Labour its own worst enemy.' *Political Quarterly,* Vol. 31, 1960, p. 374.

CRICK, Bernard, 'Socialist Literature in the 1950's.' *Political Quarterly,* Vol. 31, 1960, p. 361.

CROSLAND, C. A. R., *The Conservative Enemy.* London, 1962.

The Future of Socialism. London, 1956.

CROSSMAN, Rt Hon. Richard H. S., *Labour in the Affluent Society.* London, 1960.

Planning for Freedom. London, 1965.

Socialism and the New Despotism. London, 1956.

CYRIAX, George and Robert Oakeshott, *The Bargainers. A survey of Modern Trade Unionism.* London, 1960.

DALTON, Rt Hon. Hugh, *Call Back Yesterday.* London, 1953.

Inequality of incomes. London, 1925 (new ed.).

DANGERFIELD, George, *The Strange Death of Liberal England.* London, 1936.

DISRAELI, Rt Hon. Benjamin, Earl of Beaconsfield, *Sybil* London, 1845.

ENGEL, Friedrich, *Condition of the Working Classes in 1844. Sonnenschein.* London, 1892.

ENSOR, R. C. K., *Permeation,* quoted on p. 59 of *The Webbs and their work,* ed. M. Cole.

ESTORICK, Eric, *Stafford Cripps.* London, 1949.

FOOT, Michael, 'The age of Hazlitt', in *Tribune 21,* ed. E. Thomas, p. 152. London, 1958.

GAITSKELL, Hugh, 'The Economic Aims of the Labour Party.' *Political Quarterly,* Vol. 24, 1953.

GALTON, F. W., 'Investigating with the Webbs,' p. 30 of *The Webbs and their work,* ed. M. Cole.

GARDINER, A. G., *Pillars of Society.* London, 1916 (new ed.).

GASKELL, Mrs Elizabeth, *Mary Barton.* London, 1848.

GEORGE, Henry, *Progress and Poverty.* London, 1879.

GLASIER, J. Bruce, *William Morris and the early days of the Socialist movement.* London, 1921.

GOLLANCZ, Sir Victor, *Betrayal of the Left*. London, 1941.

GRAY, Alexander, *The Socialist Tradition, Marx to Lenin*. London, 1946.

HALDANE, Rt Hon. Richard Burdon (Lord Haldane), *An Autobiography*. London, 1929.

HAMILTON, Mary Agnes, *Sidney and Beatric Webb: a study in contemporary biography*. London, 1933.

HAMMOND, Mrs, *The Town Labourer*. London, 1950.

HANNINGTON, Wal, *The Problem of Distressed Areas*. London, 1937.

A Short History of the Unemployed. London, 1938.

HARRISSON, Tom, *see under* Madge, Charles.

HAXEY, Simon, *Tory M.P.* London, 1939.

HENDERSON, Philip Prichard, *Letters of William Morris*. London, 1950.

HERBERT, Auberon Edward William, *A Politician in trouble about his soul*. London, 1884.

HOBSBAWN, E. J., *Labour's Turning Point*. London, 1948.

HOBSON, J. A., *Imperialism*. London, 1902.

HOLYOAKE, George Jacob, *The History of the Rochdale Pioneers*. London, 1922.

HORNER, Arthur Lewis, *Incorrigible Rebel*. London, 1960.

HUGHES, Emrys, *A Biography of Keir Hardie*. London, 1956.

HUTT, Allen, *Post-war History of British Working Classes*. London, 1937.

HYNDMAN, H. M., *England for All*. London, 1881.

JAMES of Rusholme, Lord (Eric John Francis James), *Education and Leadership*. Oxford, 1961.

JENKINS, Roy Harris, *The Labour Case*. London, 1959.

Pursuit of Progress. London, 1953.

JOAD, C. E. M., (*ed.*) *Shaw and Society, an Anthology and a Symposium*. London, 1953.

JOHNSON, Paul, 'A sense of Outrage,' in *Conviction*, ed. N. Mackenzie, p. 216.

JONES, Rt Hon. Arthur Creech, *New Fabian Colonial Essays*. London, 1959.

JONES, C. S., *The Call to Liberalism*. London, 1921.

JONES, Mervyn, 'The time is short,' in *Conviction*, ed. N. Mackenzie, p. 183.

KUCSYNSKI, Jurgen, *Conditions of workers in Great Britain and Soviet Union, 1932–1938*. London, 1939.

LASKI, Harold J., *The Dilemma of our Times*. London, 1952.

Faith, Reason and Civilization. London, 1944.

A Grammar of Politics. London, 1927.

Liberty in the Modern State. London, 1930 (Pelican, 1937).

LAVERS, G. R., *see under* Rowntree, B. Seebohm.

LEWIS, Roy (and Angus Maude), *The English Middle Classes*. London, 1949.

LONDON, Jack, *People of the Abyss*. London, 1903.

LYMAN, Richard W., *The First Labour Government, 1924*. London, 1957.

MCCALLUM, Desmond, 'The Webbs as I saw them,' p. 118 of *Election of 1945*.

MACCARTHY, Desmond, '*The Webbs as I saw them*,' p. 119 of *The Webbs and their work*, ed. M. Cole.

MACCOBY, S., *English Radicalism 1886–1914*. London, 1953. *English Radicalism. The End*. London, 1961.

MACKENZIE, Norman (ed.) *Conviction*. London, 1958.

MCKENZIE, R. T., *British Political Parties*. London, 1955.

MCKITTERICK, T. E. M., 'The Membership of the Party'. *Political Quarterly*, Vol. 31, 1960, p. 312.

MADARIAGA, Don Salvador de, *Democracy versus Liberty?* London, 1958.

MADGE, Charles and Harrison, Tom, *Britain by Mass-Observation*. London, 1939.

MAHON, John A., *Trade Unionism*. London, 1938.

MARTIN, (Basil) Kingsley, *Harold Laski, A Memoir*. London, 1953.

The Webbs in Retirement.

MARX, Eleanor, *The Commonwealth*. London, 1884.

MAUDE, Angus, *see under* Lewis, Roy.

MEAD, Dr Margaret, *And keep your powder dry*. U.S.A., 1942.

MORRIS, William, *The March of the Workers* (poem).

MORTON, A. L. and Tate, George, *The British Labour Movement. 1770–1920: A History*. London, 1956.

MOULIN, Leo, *Socialism of the West*. London, 1948.

MOWAT, C. L., *Britain between the wars*. London, 1953.

MURDOCH, (Jean) Iris, 'The House of Theory,' in *Conviction*, ed. N. Mackenzie, p. 229.

NICHOLAS, H. G., *The British General Election of 1950*. London, 1951.

OAKESHOTT, Robert, *see under* Cyriax, George.

ORWELL, George, (pseud. of Eric Blair), *The Road to Wigan Pier*. London, 1937.

OSBORNE, John James, *Look Back in Anger*. London, 1956.
Subject of Scandal and Concern. London, 1960.
Plays for England. London, 1963

PARKINSON, Hargreaves, *The Ownership of Industry*. London. 1951.

PEASE, Edward R., *The History of the Fabian Society*. London, 1916.
'Webb and the Fabian Society,' *The Webbs and their Work*, ed. M. Cole, p. 24.

PELLING, Henry, *The Origins of the Labour Party, 1880–1900*. London, 1954.

PIKE, E. R., *Political Parties and Policies*. London, 1934.

PINTER, Harold, *The Birthday Party and other Plays*. London, 1960.
The Caretaker. London, 1960.

POTTER, Beatrice, *see under* Webb, Beatrice.

PRITT, Denis Nowell, *The Labour Government 1945–51*. London, 1963.

READMAN, Alison, *see under* McCallum, R. B.

ROWNTREE, B. Seebohm, *Poverty and Progress*. London, 1947.

ROWNTREE, B. Seebohm and Lavers, G. R. *Poverty and the Welfare State*. London, 1951.

SAVILLE, John (ed.), *Democracy and the Labour Movement*. London, 1954.
See also under Briggs, Asa.

SCHAFFER, Gordon, *Riches and Poverty*. London, 1939.

SCHUMPETER, J. A., *Capitalism, Socialism and Democracy*. London, 1952.

SHANKS, Michael, 'Labour Philosophy and the current position'. *Political Quarterly*, Vol. 31, 1960.

SHAW, George Bernard, *Everybody's Political What's What*. London, 1944.
Fabian Essays in Socialism. London, 1889.
The Intelligent Woman's Guide to Socialism and Capitalism. London, 1928.
Major Barbara. London, 1907.
Pen Portraits and Reviews. London, 1932.

SHORE, Peter, 'In the Room at the Top,' in *Conviction*, ed. N. Mackenzie, p. 49.

SMITH, Henry, *Economics of Socialism Reconsidered*. London, 1962.

SPENCER, Herbert, *Man versus the State*. London, 1884.

Social Statics. London, 1851 (rev. and abridged 1892).

The Study of Sociology. London, 1873.

SPENDER, J. A., *The Life of Campbell-Bannerman*. London, 1923.

The Life of Sir William Harcourt, quoted in Sidney and Beatrice Webb, M. A. Hamilton.

Life of Asquith, Earl of Oxford. London, 1932.

SPENDER, Stephen (Harold), *Forward from Liberalism.* London, 1937.

STRACHEY, John, *Contemporary Capitalism.* London, 1956.

A Faith to Fight For. London, 1941.

'The Object of Further Socialisation'. *Political Quarterly*, Vol. 24, 1953, p. 6.

The Theory and Practice of Socialism. London, 1936.

Why you should be a Socialist. London, 1945.

TATE, George, *see under* Morton, A. L.

TAWNEY, R. H., *Equality.* London, 1952 (new ed.).

The Attack. London, 1953.

The Webbs in Perspective. London, 1953.

THOMAS, Elizabeth, *Tribune 21.* London, 1958.

THOMPSON, E. P. (ed.), *Out of Apathy.* London, 1966.

William Morris: Romantic to Revolutionary. London, 1955.

TOWNSEND, Peter, 'A Society for People,' in *Conviction,* ed. N. Mackenzie, p. 96.

VERNON, Anne, *Joseph Rowntree.* London, 1958.

VIPONT, Elfrida, *Arnold Rowntree.* London, 1955.

WALLAS, Graham, *Human Nature in Politics.* London, 1908.

WARD, Maisie, *Gilbert Keith Chesterton.* London, 1944.

WEARMOUTH, Robert R., *The Social and Political Influence of Methodism in the Twentieth Century.* London, 1957.

WEBB, Beatrice, *The Co-Operative Movement of Great Britain.* London, 1891 (2nd ed. 1893).

Report on the Poor Law. London, 1909.

My Apprenticeship. 2 vols. Pelican, London, 1938.

Our Partnership (ed. B. Drake and M. Cole). London, 1948.

WEBB, Sidney James (Lord Passfield), *The History of Trade Unionism.* London, 1894.

Industrial Democracy. London, 1897.

Labour and the New Social Order, lecture 8 Nov. 1901, quoted in Pelling, H., op. cit.

Labour in the Longest Reign. 1837–1897. London, 1897.

Basis and Policy of Socialism. London, 1908.

WEBB, Sidney and Beatrice, *A Constitution for the British Socialist Commonwealth*. London, 1920.

WELLS, H. G., *The New Machiavelli*. London, 1911.
A Modern Utopia. London, 1905.

WESKER, Arnold, *Chips with Everything*. London, 1962.
Roots. London, 1959.
I'm talking about Jerusalem. London, 1960.

WILDE, Oscar, *The Soul of Man Under Socialism*. London, 1912 (privately printed in 1895).

WILKINSON, Ellen, *The Town that was Murdered*. London, 1939.

WILLIAMS, Lord Francis, *Ernest Bevin, Portrait of a Great Englishman*. London, 1952.

WILSON, Rt Hon. Harold, *Purpose in Politics*. London, 1964.
The Relevance of British Socialism. London, 1964.

WOOLF, Leonard, *Political Thought and the Webbs*. Quoted in *The Webbs and their work*, ed. M. Cole, p. 59.

YATES, Ivan, 'Power in the Labour Party'. *Political Quarterly*, Vol. 31, 1960, p. 300.

YOUNG, Wayland and Elizabeth, *The Socialist Imagination*. London, 1960.

ZWEIG, F., *Labour, Life and Poverty*. London, 1948.

INDEX